YEARNING *for* NORMAL

Gold Medal Reader's Favorite Award 2014, Non-fiction, Christian Living category

...Above all, however, this book shows the power of love and compassion, which makes life meaningful and valuable in the face of threats that most of us face at one stage or another in our lives. Highly recommended for everyone who values life and love. Ernest Demsey, Word Matters http://www.ernestdempsey.com/?s=yearning+for+normal

I read this book in 4 hrs... Could not put it down. Incredible story told with such raw honesty. As a PT, I have been on the other side of that hospital bed, other side of the table at the IEP meeting, and been on those home visits. This story is such a good reminder for all health care workers to consider the entire journey, take time to learn each person's story, and truly treat the patient and the family.
Amber McCreary
http://www.amazon.com/Yearning-Normal-Susan-Ellison-Busch/product-reviews/1625106726/

Susan's open, honest writing about her life with her son is encouraging not only to those in similar situations, but to all of us who are finding our way through life. Most of all, her chapter on forgiveness is so powerful that all if us should read it. This book is an amazing story of redemption.
Leigh Ann
https://www.goodreads.com/book/show/18179250-yearning-for-normal?from_search=true

YEARNING *for* NORMAL

Learning Acceptance

SUSAN ELLISON BUSCH

Gray Horse
PRESS

Published by Grey Horse Press. Books may be purchased for educational, business, or sales promotional use. For information, please write: Sales Department. 280 Kendall Park Rd, Peninsula, Ohio 44264

Library of Congress Control Number: 2015901595

Published in the United States of America

ISBN: 978-0-692-37329-3
1. Family & Relationships / Children With Special Needs
2. Spirituality

DEDICATION

For my son, Mike,
a major prophet in my life,
in teaching me about God
and teaching me over and over again how to love.

ACKNOWLEDGMENTS

Thank you to my kind friends and family members for your encouragement in reading, editing, and commenting on the early versions: Celeste Jindra and her book club, Mary Jindra, Catherine Hershey, Pam VanSiclen, Anne Dorley, Tim Ellison, Dave Ellison, Mary Holden, Jac Pearl, Anne Lawlor, Sherry Baker-Gomez, Annie and Kurt Haberl, David Busch, and Richard Schneider. Your love and support are appreciated more than I can say. Thank you also to my two editors, Lindsey Marcus and Kathleen Dupré.

CONTENTS

INTRODUCTION

Every creature is a word of God and is a book
about God.[1]

Meister Eckhart

M ichael, my son was born missing a submicroscopic piece of chromosome 22. That tiny missing fragment of DNA affected every aspect of his life physically, mentally, and spiritually. It affected not only his life but also the lives of our entire family, his friends, neighbors, and the students in the schools he attended. This is the story of my journey as Mike's mother. This story needs to be told. There are many families living similar stories. Though we now know that the cause of my son's struggles was a tiny missing piece of chromosome, we did not know that for many of his growing-up years. Discovering the cause of his illnesses and problems is part of the story.

There are many names for the constellation of symptoms caused by this missing piece of chromosome.

Some of them include: Velocardiofacial syndrome (VCFS), DiGeorge Syndrome, 22q11.2 Deletion Syndrome, Sprintzen Syndrome, Catch 22 syndrome, Conotruncal anomaly face syndrome (CTAF), Opitz G/BBB Syndrome, and Caylor cardiofacial syndrome. Probably all of those terms sound strange and exotic, leading to the belief that it is a rare occurrence. In reality, chromosome 22 misplaces this fragment frequently. It occurs every four thousand births or so. This syndrome is almost as common as Down syndrome; however, most doctors, nurses, schoolteachers, social workers, and therapists, who care for individuals with this deletion in the course of their daily work, have not even heard of it. For the sake of simplicity, I will refer to Michael's syndrome as 22q.11 Deletion Syndrome, but any of the other names listed above refer to the same missing piece of chromosome. Some people give this syndrome the nickname "22q."

The idea for writing this story came as my son Mike was hovering between life and death in the burn unit of our local hospital. As I sat at his bedside, I wrote e-mail updates to my friends. A few encouraged me to put his story in a book. As I started writing, I realized that the burn, harrowing as it was, was just a chapter in the larger story of my son's life and struggles as a person with 22q.11 Deletion Syndrome. Much of his life leading up to that point had been a perilous journey.

My main purpose for writing the book is to increase the conversation and awareness of 22q.11 Deletion Syndrome in the general society. Another purpose is to teach people who care for children with this syndrome professionally about some of the issues that parents deal with. I also hope to encourage the parents of children with 22q.11 Deletion Syndrome. I think if I'd had a book like this when I was a young mother, I would not have felt as alone as I struggled with so many issues. I wanted to know that someone else had been where I was, and knew my struggles first hand. This is not a how-to-book, though. At best it is a cautionary tale.

Though each child is different with unique problems and concerns, for parents, the heart issues are similar: the fears, the sorrows, the hopes, and wishes for our children. I am hoping that readers will feel encouraged by my mistakes in loving, by my insecurities, and by my wrestling matches with God. Perhaps parents will not feel so alone or crazy when contending for their child's benefit, with the educational and health care systems in place today. Many of the stories in this book will be familiar to parents who have children with this deletion. I hope in the sharing of this story that parents of children with 22q.11 Deletion Syndrome find a kindred spirit or mentor in me as they struggle with so many issues in raising their children.

As I started writing, I found it difficult to make a clean separation between this story, and many of the other stories intertwining with it. Perhaps it is so with all our stories. Each of our smaller stories intertwines, coalesces, and converges into one grand old story told by the Master Storyteller. It is through our stories that we grow and come to know who we are and who

God is. We tell our stories to entertain but also to understand ourselves, teach ourselves, and teach each other. A Hasidic parable explains that the reason God created man was because He loved stories.[2] This is a messy story, as most true stories are.

Since this story is part of a larger one, it is not just for the parents of children with 22q.11 Deletion syndrome, but for their friends, neighbors, doctors, nurses, teachers, speech therapists, physical therapists, social workers, police officers, firefighters, ministers, and whoever else likes a good story. This story is also for those who have watched someone they love suffer, and felt hopeless and powerless, wondering where God was in the midst of the pain.

At the very least, I hope that the reader will acquire different eyes when seeing someone perhaps emptying the garbage, or wiping tables at Burger King. Usually these ancillary people are invisible or on the periphery of our own stories, but perhaps after reading this story, the reader will start to see the rich stories that these people or those who know and love them could tell.

Readers hoping to learn about the current scientific understandings of the deletion will be disappointed. This book skims over most clinical and scientific information. Research findings are snowballing at a much faster rate than this book could be written or published. There are many research articles statistically analyzing and categorizing many of the medical, psychiatric, genetic, and educational issues associated with 22q.11 Deletion Syndrome. Research papers have limitations though. Numbers rarely tell the full story. Numbers approach a subject from the outside. This book tells the story from the inside.

In telling the story, I also attempt to illuminate some of my spiritual questions and struggles. As Mike's mother, I became an amateur theologian, considering and struggling with many questions that probably would not have even occurred to me if it were not for Mike. It is when people are on the edge that they start wrestling with eternal questions. Parenting a child with 22q.11 Deletion Syndrome has the potential to take parents to the edge, many times over the edge. Parents not only struggle with questions of, "What is the best treatment for this medical problem?" and "What is the best way to educate my child?", but also with questions of, "How do we get through today?", "Why did this happen to our family?", and "Where is God in the midst of all this mess?" I know many parents with special-needs children feel guilt and shame on top of all the other struggles. I hope to help in some way to free them from that sinkhole.

I struggled with the idea of whether to include my theological ramblings in this book—vacillating between the opinions that they either distracted or added to the story. I kept them in, thinking that if someone was bored or annoyed with the content, they could skim over it and still enjoy a good story.

I wrote this book not only from a mother's perspective, but also with the eyes and heart of a nurse. I worked for most of Michael's childhood as a dialysis nurse before becoming a nurse practitioner. Having a nurse for a mother had benefits and burdens for Mike. The poor kid grew up with a mom who pulled out a stethoscope every time he coughed or wheezed. By the time he was four years old, he had learned to run away howling as fast as he could when he saw me walk to the stethoscope drawer. My nursing knowledge was helpful at times; other times it interfered with his care.

Just as there are many stories and stories within stories, there are also many points of view, different stories of the same story. I could not write this book from the perspective of my son, Michael, my husband, Art, or other sons, Benjamin and David. Though we have lived these stories and years together, the stories from their perspectives are different. If I tried to tell their stories in addition to my story, this book would never be published and would be thousands of pages long. I hope that explains their cameo appearances in this book. I tell these stories as a mother, but in reality, we all lived these stories as a family. Mike however, has made a few contributions to the book. He wants people to understand his feelings about what he went through.

My one fear is that young parents, reading about some of the more difficult parts of the story, might become afraid. Do not be afraid. Just take the journey one day at a time and trust. Remember, the grace to deal with whatever crisis comes along presents itself only when and if the crisis appears. I am grateful for all we have been through, no matter how sordid or difficult, because each crisis has taught us to love a little better, and has opened our eyes to see a little more of reality.

Mikey's older brother Ben thought stethoscopes were as much a part of baby care as bottles and diapers

THE AMBULANCE RIDE

All sorrows can be borne if you tell a story
about them.[3]

Karen Blixen

I entered the back door, crossed the threshold to
our kitchen, and discovered my twenty-two-year-
old son Mike, standing stark naked, hands covering
his genitals. The lights were off in the kitchen, and
he stood in the grey twilight of a mid-March early
evening. His eyes were wide with fear. Black flakes were
scattered over his torso. The question, "What is that
stuck on your skin?" squeaked out of my mouth. Then,
as I looked closer and saw his singed hair, I moaned,
"Oh God, you are burned!"

I phoned for an ambulance. As I called, Mike paced
back and forth in the kitchen saying, "Just drive me.
I'll be okay." He told me that he had been cooking
meatballs and his shirt caught on fire. While waiting
for the ambulance, I got him some pants for modesty,

covering his burnt waist and buttocks. I remembered a little from nursing school about burns, so I tried to get him to lie down on a quilt since I knew he was in danger of going into shock.

He was too restless to lie down and just kept pacing. He was in a lot of pain. He finally sat down on the couch to wait. As he rocked back and forth, I sat next to him—afraid to touch him for fear of causing more pain to his burns. The house was smoky, and his clothes were still smoldering in piles that he had ripped off on his fiery dash to the shower.

The ambulance arrived. I got a better look at his burns as the paramedics helped him to the stretcher. The skin of his upper torso was lightly browned, leathery. There were holes in it where you could see some of the fatty layer of skin underneath. It reminded me of the skin on a roasting chicken. His ears were white. As the paramedics got ready to transport Mike, they took his vital signs, started an IV, and gave him morphine.

I recognized one of the paramedics from many previous emergency transports. He had first transported Mike on several runs as a baby, then as an adolescent, and now as an adult. The paramedic had been a young man once, but now he was balding and had crow's feet around his eyes. He provided the same earnest care and kind smile.

As they got Mike prepared for transport, I grabbed my purse, jacket, and a book—a reflex habit acquired after innumerable hours spent in hospital ERs and doctors' waiting rooms. I did not realize that it would be weeks before I would be able to focus on anything long enough to read. On some level, I knew that the burn was serious, but the fact that he was walking and talking gave me a sense of security, that maybe the situation really wasn't that awful.

Later, while chatting with the nurses who cared for Mike, I discovered that after a severe burn there is a one-to-two-hour grace period before shock and collapse set in. One of the burn nurses told me the story of an Amish mother whose kerosene heater exploded in the basement while she was refinishing some furniture. She and her three young children caught fire.

Though 80 percent of her body had been burned, she put out the fire in the basement and on each of her children. She cleansed and clothed each of the children and then changed her own clothes before trudging barefoot in the winter snow across many fields to the nearest phone to call for help. When the ambulance arrived at her house, she was sitting in a rocking chair, nursing her baby. Yet, by the time the helicopter arrived at the hospital burn unit thirty minutes later, she was in shock and full cardiac arrest. Her baby was dead.

The ambulance transporting Mike arrived at the hospital. They rushed Mike's stretcher past the Emergency Room, directly to the burn unit. I walked next to Mike's stretcher. He was talking to me and was worried about the pants that I had insisted he put on. The paramedics had cut them off, and he was wondering what he would wear home that night.

The nurses yelled at the paramedics for bringing him straight to the burn unit without stopping in the Emergency Room, and then directed me to Admitting. I walked down a long, dark hall, turning many corners in the dimly lit maze of hospital corridors. In Admitting, a lone, middle-aged woman sat in the shadows at a desk in a cubicle. I had entered "The Twilight Zone." The admitting process took forever. Reality sank in. Time stopped. The receptionist's questions and typing took on a surreal, slow-motion quality. I just wanted to be back by Mike's side and to see how he was doing. I knew he could die.

Once she finished her infernal, eternal paperwork, I rushed back to the triage room where they were working on Mike. The nurses exiled me to the waiting room. I tried to explain that I was a nurse, that nothing would make me faint, and that Mike would feel more secure with me around. No luck.

As I waited alone in the silent, semi-dark waiting room, I watched the nurses and techs run in and out of the triage room, bringing tubes of blood, requesting this or that tray. While I sat there, I called my friends from my cell phone. A dear friend of mine burst into tears when she heard. Our children had played many hours together since they were very young. Her tears comforted me more than any words could, and I wept too, not knowing what the future held. My husband arrived a little later, and we waited in silence, bound together by our fear and sorrow.

Sometime later, the resident on call came to take a patient history and let us know what to expect. We told him that Mike had Velocardiofacial Syndrome (VCFS). He hadn't heard of that, so we told him he had DiGeorge Syndrome. He hadn't heard of that either, so we told him that our son had a tiny deletion of chromosome 22. The resident had no idea what that meant either.

When health care providers take a patient history, they are hoping for a very short, concise story of what has happened in the past to the patient in order to guide their care and anticipate any problems they might encounter. It had been a long and circuitous journey to the understanding that a tiny, submicroscopic deletion of chromosome 22 had caused a host of odd medical problems, developmental abnormalities, social and learning difficulties—and more recently—psychiatric illness, which was the direct cause of the burn, you will find out later.

To tell the story of Mike's life with all its adventures and intertwining and supporting stories would fill a book or at least take all night. It would be a fascinating story, except for the fact that he is our son. No one hopes for interesting medical histories involving their children or those they love.

We gave the resident a condensed version because we didn't want to keep him even for one extra moment from taking care of our son. However, for you, the reader, pull up a chair and open your heart. I have a story to tell you.

THE JOURNEY BEGINS

All journeys have secret destinations of which
the traveler is unaware.[4]

Martin Buber

I lay on the exam table, my legs spread-eagled in stirrups, as the grandfatherly obstetrician rummaged through my internal organs. He was sitting on a stool, and the drapes over my legs blocked his face from my view. I stared at the water stains on the ceiling tiles, afraid of what he might find. I had been feeling so lousy after the miscarriage. After scouring all my nursing textbooks for post-miscarriage illnesses, I had concluded that either there were retained "products of conception" festering inside me, or I was now dying of some rare disease.

The doctor popped his head above the drape, with a big grin on his face.

"I have discovered the source of your symptoms. You, my dear, are still pregnant."

I whipped my feet out of the stirrups, sat up quickly, and looked at him quizzically. "Pregnant! How can that be?"

He tilted his head, looked at me with a smirk on his face, and asked, "You don't know where babies come from?"

I groaned at his teasing. "You know what I mean… the second pregnancy test was negative." Initially, I had a positive pregnancy test, and then I bled. Thinking I had an early miscarriage, I took another over-the-counter pregnancy test a week later, and the results were negative.

"I don't know. I suspect that you just had a period after becoming pregnant—that happens sometimes. It is also possible that the second pregnancy test was defective." He speculated. He wrote a prescription for a pre-natal vitamin, and I made a follow-up appointment for the following month.

I walked out of his office and into the warm October breeze. The trees clapped their hands and showered a confetti of leaves on me and the little life inside. I felt jubilant and like a complete idiot at the same time. All my symptoms made sense now. I remembered feeling this terrible with my firstborn son, but the context was different. I knew I was pregnant at that time, and understood the headaches, nausea, vomiting, and extreme fatigue to be common symptoms during the first few months. This time, because I believed that I had miscarried early on in the pregnancy, there hadn't been the same context to put the symptoms in. I am a nurse, and I should have known better, but my objectivity gets lost easily when dealing with my own illnesses. In retrospect, this confusion about the pregnancy was an apt beginning for a life filled with questions and bewilderment.

This doctor's office was close to my father's office; so on the way home, I stopped by to tell him the good news. As soon as I finished telling him, he frowned.

"Why are you having another one so close to the first one?" he asked.

"I don't know," I shrugged. "I sort of liked growing up with siblings close to my age." We weren't just siblings; we were friends. There was always someone to play with or fight with.

To be honest, though, there was nothing of the sort in my calculations. This pregnancy was an accident. I had a fourteen-month-old son at home who had just started walking. Planned or unplanned, most pregnancies carry with them a certain amount of ambivalence. Every pregnancy is a journey into the unknown. An expectant mother is bringing a new human being into the world. Who is this person going to be? It could be a Hitler or a Gandhi. Certainly, this mystery person will change every relationship in the mother's world.

When I was pregnant with my firstborn son, I ruminated that that was the first relationship in my life I could not abandon. I could not send this person back if I did not like him or her. I also struggled with many fears. I was afraid of labor. I wondered if I was even "mother material." (I could not keep houseplants alive. How in the world could a little living human survive with my nurturing skill set?) So many fears and anxieties churned in my heart as he churned in my abdomen.

We named our firstborn Benjamin. When he was born, I was born simultaneously as someone else, a new mother. Looking at him the day he was born, I was surprised and amazed at the ferocious love and responsibility I experienced for this tiny, helpless human's welfare and safety. I remember feelings of awe as I walked to the nursery window and looked at him. What had started as a simple act of love had become a living human being.

Something big inside of me shifted. It was the first moment in my life that I was glad to be a woman. Before then, I had been convinced that men had the better deal in life. (For the most part, they did have a better deal in the 1970s. They could play sports, they could serve on the altar in the Catholic Church I was raised in, and they could do or be anything they wanted to be.) However, the moment I saw my firstborn, everything changed. My woman's body had brought a new life into the world. As I marveled at him, I experienced a bond of sisterhood and motherhood with every woman alive, who had ever lived, and who was still to come.

That magical, mystical experience of sharing motherhood with the universe quickly dissipated with the shock of bringing an infant home. I was distressed to discover that my time and my days were no longer my own. My days were at his service. Not only that, he had colic and didn't like sleeping at night. There were some days during those first few weeks when my husband would arrive home from work to find me still in my pajamas and crying because I had not been able to get a single thing accomplished the entire day, let alone take a shower. Ben would also be crying. After a few weeks, though, things improved. I relaxed a little. I developed routines, managing to take showers and get dressed. As I settled into motherhood, I learned to attend to his needs and started to love the moments of his babyhood. I started learning the long lesson that my value as a mother did not depend on what I accomplished each day, but on the love brought to the chaos of the broken and disconnected moments. I grew to love being a mother.

Now I was pregnant again. I was not afraid of labor this time. Nothing could be as bad as that first one, and as bad as it was, it was worth it. This time the question that churned in my mind was, "How is it possible to love two babies?" I loved Benjamin totally. How could I split this absolute love with another baby?

Jumbled in with the ambivalence of pregnancy, there was also a secret joy at the privilege of bringing life into this world. Just the idea of being pregnant, with all its possibilities, is an adventure. As the baby and I grew in size, I believed that this one must be a girl because there was much less movement and kicking than I had experienced with my firstborn son. I imagined a dainty, quiet, little girl who would snuggle and read books with me.

From the moment I knew I was pregnant, already loving the fragile, little life inside me, I would place my hands on my womb and pray for God to bless the baby developing within me and keep whoever it was strong and healthy. I recited the part of Psalm 139 that describes God watching our bones take shape as we are knitted together in secret in our mother's womb. (Psalm 139:15).

To give a little background on the nature of my faith during those days, I was raised a traditional Roman Catholic. I learned to approach God through ritual, liturgy, and jumping through hoops. If a person jumped through the basic hoops, he would go to heaven; if he jumped through the second or third tiers of hoops, he or she could possibly become a saint. Even as a child, though, I had this hint of a personal God, a friend who smiled at me from behind the curtains of the tabernacle in church.

One Friday night when I was in my teens, a close friend brought me to a Bible study with a group of hippie Christians. For those readers old enough to remember, they were Jesus Freaks. I went because I was curious how people could think it was fun to study the Bible on a Friday night. In the fellowship, worship, prayer, and study though, I encountered Jesus. He was no longer a distant God peaking at me from His hiding place, but a Living Presence closer to me than I was to myself. I learned that God did not require hoops. The Divinity that created rambling universes, for some strange reason wanted a love relationship with all of us. The Bible became real when I was baptized in the Holy Spirit and spoke in tongues. I discovered that the words in scripture were living and true. Scripture was not *just* a bunch of old stories. The main gift I received when I became a new Christian was an absolute hunger for God that has been the hallmark of all my living and seeking since then. I began to see everything that happened during my days both large and small in light of my relationship with God. That is why it is impossible to separate my story as the mother of Mike from my story as a friend of God.

I became a rabid fundamentalist. I knew everything. I had faith. That was a time of many miracles and answered prayers. It was a good place to start, but my understanding has changed many times since then. In fact, over the years I have discovered that I have fewer and fewer answers, but perhaps I am asking better questions.

Our second son was born close to midnight on April 12, 1983. When he was born, his Apgar was 10, meaning that all the signs they assess in the first minutes after birth were perfect. (That was the last time in his life that he scored a perfect 10 on anything.) They bundled him up and placed him in my arms. He didn't cry; he just looked at me and whimpered. I smiled at his cute, little face and whispered, "Don't cry, my beautiful, wonderful son. You are here. Welcome home." The obstetrician looked at me, shook his head, and insisted, "Oh no, it's good when they cry. We want him to cry!"

We named him Michael. His name comes from Michael the archangel, the one who fought with Satan. It means "one who is like God."

A few weeks later, when the pediatrician learned that we had named him Michael, he started clucking his tongue with a little smirk on his face, "Never, never, never name a child Michael!" It was a little late for him to be telling me at that point. When I asked why, he replied, "Michaels are nothing but trouble." He was kidding, and yet quite serious at the same time. Other people have told me "Michael" stories over the years, confirming the pediatrician's bias. Michael was the right name for our son, though—not so much for all the trouble, but because he has been "one like God" in challenging us to grow and change in so many ways, and teaching us to look below the surface, teaching us to love unconditionally.

Then the doctor delivered the placenta. He remarked that there was something wrong with it, and then I hemorrhaged. The doctor called for help in the delivery room. One nurse whisked Mikey away, while another gave me a shot of Pitocin in my left thigh to constrict my uterus and stop the bleeding. I remember the shot, and then I remember floating up and away, feeling exhilarated, so light and free and joyful, no need to carry this heavy body around anymore. It was the most peaceful experience of my life to date. I cannot say if this was one of those edge-of-life experiences or if I just passed out, but I distinctly remember thinking of my new son and deciding I had better return.

The next thing I knew, I was awake, and they had IVs in my arms and a swarm of medical personnel working on me. One held a mask to my face, compressing the oxygen bag to keep me breathing. My husband, who was present, said that it looked like I had had a seizure before passing out.

They worked on me a little longer, before transferring me to my hospital room with padded side rails. (Nurses pad side rails with blankets when someone has had a seizure, in case they might have another one in the bed. This way the metal rails won't cause any bruising.) My husband went home to sleep and care for Mikey's older brother, Ben.

Once in my room and medically stable, I kept asking the nurses to bring in my son, so I could see him and hug him and count his toes. I remembered those delicious early hours with my firstborn and wanted to bond with Mikey. I hungered to see him. The nurses would respond to my call light, but when I asked to have my son brought to me, they disappeared. I waited and waited and waited and waited as I slept fitfully. I assumed they weren't bringing my son because they were afraid I might have another seizure.

Early the following morning, an entourage of doctors, residents, and interns filed into my hospital room to tell me that my baby was in the Neonatal Intensive Care Unit (NICU) at the children's hospital. They had discovered a problem with his heart. In front of the gawking group, I burst into tears, the first of buckets for Mike since then. In Psalm 56:8 (JB) there is a line, "You

collect my tears in your wineskin." To contain the lifetime of my tears shed for Mike, God's wineskin needs
to be as large as a water tower or small lake.

A short time later, the cardiologist returned. He
gently described Michael's condition and drew pictures
of the problem with his heart. He told me that in the
first hour of life, Mikey's lungs had filled with fluid, and
he had started having difficulty breathing. The doctor
told me Mikey had pulmonary hypertension (too much
pressure in the artery leading from the right side of the
heart to the lungs) and coarctation of the aorta. This is
a narrowing or kinking of the main artery that comes
out of his heart. He believed Mikey would be needing
surgery in the first few months of life.

An underground tunnel connected the maternity
hospital to the children's hospital where Mikey was in
the NICU. They took me in a wheelchair to see him.
Mikey was in an isolette, attached to a heart monitor,
with an IV in his scalp and so many tubes. I wasn't able
to pick him up and hold him. I could only look. The
act of giving birth tears apart a woman's insides. Seeing
Mikey in this condition ripped my insides again—a
deep, visceral, spiritual pain. That particular maternal
wound has never quite healed. I also learned at that
moment that love is infinite. There was no need to
worry about sharing it or splitting up the love between
two sons.

UNANSWERED PRAYERS

We were promised sufferings. They were
part of the program. We were even told,
"blessed are they that mourn."[5]

C.S. Lewis

After I learned about Mikey's heart problem, I
didn't lose faith or stop praying or talking to
God, but a few, basic theological underpinnings needed
some adjustment.

I asked, "Lord, remember when I would place my
hands on my womb and pray for his health and safety?
What did you do with those prayers?"

"Did you purposely create him with the heart defect,
or was it something outside of your control?"

"Were you really watching, or did you get distracted
with the responsibility of holding all the galaxies on
their courses?"

"Were my prayers impotent, or are you impotent?"

"I thought we had an understanding here…"

"I am not angry or anything, just wondering…"

Since this simple prayer hadn't been answered, I started wondering about all the other prayers of mine that were still floating about the universe unanswered. A crack opened between what I believed was faith and the reality I faced. Mikey's birth marked the beginning of a long, drawn-out wrestling match between God and me.

Recently, when I was encouraging my older son Ben to pray and seek for guidance for his life, he looked at me and said, "Mom, everyone prays; it's just that we don't always know who or what it is we are praying to." It is when we suffer, or God seems silent, that people start grappling with the question, "Who is this 'Hidden One' behind the curtain of creation?" Is this divinity personally involved with our lives, or is the world set on autopilot and the chips fall as they may? No one who lives long enough on this earth is immune from the problem of unanswered prayers.

Reading about Jesus's unanswered prayers is how I learned to sit with my own unanswered prayer for a healthy child. Jesus, in His agony in the garden the night before His crucifixion, asked to have the cup of suffering removed from Him. He asked for life, for a different story, for a way out. He may have hoped for the same reprieve Abraham received when God substituted a goat for His son. That prayer wasn't answered. As Jesus hung dying on the cross, He wailed, "My God, my God, why have you deserted me?" (Matthew 27:46, jb).

Jesus also has another, very large, unanswered prayer. At the Passover Seder the night before He died, as His disciples were arguing over who was the best and Peter, His chosen leader, was refusing to have his feet washed, and His friend Judas was plotting His betrayal, Jesus prayed that all those who believed in Him would be one just as He and the Father are one. He prayed that His followers would love each other. He prayed that the unity of believers would be a witness to the world of the love the Father has for us (John 17:20-22). As far as I can tell, Jesus is still waiting for an answer to that prayer.

Much of church history is sadly a story of cataclysm, bloodshed, and division among the followers of Jesus—all professing to have the market on orthodoxy. Now from my perspective, that is pathetic—two thousand years and we are still deriding each other and fighting over fine points of doctrine. However, God is God. This creation is close to eighteen billion years old, according to our best scientific estimates. In God's timetable, it has only been a few seconds. Perhaps things are progressing as planned.

Coincidentally, the book I grabbed to bring with me to the hospital for Mikey's birth was *Why do Bad Things Happen to Good People?* by Rabbi Harold S. Kushner.[6] Rabbi Kushner began a quest similar to mine when he had a son who died from a premature aging disease called Progeria. His son died of old age when he was fourteen.

Instead of blaming original sin, the Christian explanation for suffering based on the story in the third chapter of Genesis, Kushner approached the problem of suffering using the story of creation found in the two chapters of Genesis. In this story, creation begins when the earth was just chaos, a dark, formless wasteland over which the Spirit of God hovered. This chapter goes on to explain how God, in creation, created order out of chaos and darkness. On the sixth day, God created humankind in His own image and likeness. And God saw that it was good and rested and blessed the Sabbath.

Rabbi Kushner suggested that perhaps it is not yet the Sabbath. Perhaps it is just Friday afternoon. Even the scientific findings of our day corroborate this idea of continuing creation. The Hubble telescope, which has identified two hundred billion galaxies like our own Milky Way, continues to reveal new galaxies and stars birthed daily. This understanding of continuing creation is not just found in the Hebrew Scriptures. It is also found in the New Testament. Paul, in the book of Romans, states, "From the beginning till now the entire creation, as we know, has been groaning in one great act of giving birth" (Romans 8:22, JB).

It is comforting to consider that creation is still in process. God's words continue to create order out of chaos, waste, and void. When God created us in His image and likeness and gave us dominion over the rest of creation, He also gave us the power to become co-creators with him in bringing life and light to areas that are still dark and void (even those areas within our own hearts).

In this worldview, suffering and calamity are part of the chaos over which the Spirit of God hovers. There is no sense in asking the question, "Why did God allow this to happen?" The question changes to, "Where do I find the Spirit of God hovering over this mess?" or "How do I partner with God in creating love and light in this situation?" The disadvantage of this worldview is that things are a little less secure. Prayer and faith do not insure protection from evil and illness and calamity.

I do not believe for a moment that I have this amazing creation figured out, or that it is possible to explain suffering in this world. We live our lives in mystery. A molecule of creation understood only distracts from the millions of rambling universes not even imagined.

I realize the past few pages were a major digression from the story, but I felt that it was important because over the years, as the mother of a person with a disability, I have encountered many people who assert and believe that because they have faith, their children will be healthy and nothing bad will happen to them. This is dangerous theology, because what happens to faith when calamity strikes?

It is also dangerous because of the undercurrents it creates. People would never state flatly the foolish belief that bad things happen because God loves someone less, and yet underneath—under the surface—the questions abound. Sometimes over the years, I found myself feeling a little less loved by God when struggling with so many issues and problems. It took a long time to reach the place where I came to understand that God in His love wants us to grow into a trust in Him that goes deeper than circumstances or answered prayers.

SO MANY QUESTIONS

Live your questions now, and perhaps even
without knowing it, you will live along some
distant day into your answers.[7]

Ranier Maria Rilke

Everyone I knew was praying for Mikey. After a few
days in the NICU, Mikey stabilized; his breathing
improved, and they let me nurse him. He had difficulty
nursing and tired easily with sucking. It was an expected
glitch, given his heart problems. A few days later, we
brought him home from the hospital. Those first few
months, my husband and I noticed some odd little quirks
about him. As a newborn, he would always sleep with
his neck tilted back. His cry was weak and hoarse, and
he would turn blue around his mouth when he cried.
His breathing was noisy. He would get restless and start
struggling to breathe whenever he was placed flat after
eating. It was part-mother instinct, part-nurse instinct,
but I quickly learned that he needed to be in an upright

position after eating. He spent most of his infancy in an umbrella stroller or infant seat. Even for nighttime sleeping, he was often more comfortable in a semi-upright position. At the time, in my ignorance, I attributed this phenomenon to orthopnea. Orthopnea is a symptom of heart failure in adults where it is hard to breathe when lying flat. In retrospect, it was more likely due to the reflux of his stomach contents into his esophagus and possibly into his lungs when he was lying flat.

After a few months, his heart improved, and the cardiologist felt that he no longer needed surgery for the coarctation of the aorta. In fact, he was not even sure Mikey had it anymore. The pulmonary hypertension had also resolved when the fluid cleared from his lungs. I remember feeling hopeful as the cardiologist held little Mikey in his arms and exclaimed, "Such a beautiful baby!" He was a beautiful baby.

However, he didn't grow and gain weight as expected. He started life in the fiftieth percentile and should have stayed in that range throughout childhood, but by his third month of life, he had dropped to the third percentile. I knew that I was not making as much milk as I had with my first son because Mikey had difficulties sucking, so I supplemented breast feeding by experimenting with various formulas.

Other puzzling problems arose during those early months. He was always constipated. He couldn't move his bowels without a suppository. The stock boy at the local pharmacy probably wondered why the infant suppository jars that usually gathered dust were suddenly disappearing from the shelves. I tried to describe this problem with the constipation to the pediatrician. It seemed rather drastic and extreme to me. She just dismissed it.

The pediatrician was more concerned about him being a "floppy baby." Mikey lacked the muscle tone that normal babies have. He missed the normal infant developmental milestones. Mikey was quite the mellow baby. He may have been a little too placid. I have a friend who had a baby who was born within weeks of Mikey. Sometimes when he was just at home with us, it was easy to pretend that he was unique but normal, but when we placed him in his infant seat next to my friend's baby, denial was a little more difficult. My friend's baby would be craning her neck and trying to gather in all of life and activity, struggling to get out of the infant seat, and Mikey would be sitting quietly, just breathing and looking.

I hated taking Mikey for the routine well-baby checkups. He wasn't a well-baby, and nothing was routine. Frequently, I came home from a routine well-baby visit in tears after his doctor had suggested a new diagnosis, test, or specialist. Sometimes it was a minor problem; other times it was ominous. One time, she was all concerned that his skin was taking on a yellow cast. Under some lights, he looked a little jaundiced. That could have been a serious sign of liver disease, but it was caused only by the amount of carrots, sweet potatoes, and peaches he consumed. He loved eating yellow and orange food. He must have needed Vitamin

A for some reason. I was delighted to feed him anything he would eat.

Mikey munching on a yellow peach

Another issue was that Mikey had a tendency to develop infections, from pneumonias and sinus infections to bladder and fungal skin infections. We lived in crisis. The first two years of his life, Mikey had pneumonia more times than I can count. A pulmonologist who saw him when he was around two years old reviewed all the chest x-rays that he had had at that particular hospital. He told me that Mikey had never had a normal chest x-ray. After performing a bronchoscopy, another pulmonologist told me he had never seen a trachea so floppy (it is supposed to be stiff), or the bronchial tubes branched in the manner his were.

When Mikey first started walking, he was clumsier than most; he was always falling and bumping his head. The pediatrician, seeing his bruises, hinted that she was concerned I abused him—that is, until she saw him fall twice and bump his head in her office. She then dropped that line of questioning.

During one of his hospitalizations for failure to thrive, the staff weighed him daily to see if he gained weight in the hospital. They suspected he was so little because I wasn't feeding him enough. One day, when they weighed him with a diaper on, when the previous day they had weighed him with the diaper off, an intern came in and presented me with the evidence of his weight gain in the hospital. He insinuated that perhaps Mikey was so small because I wasn't feeding him at home. I became enraged and told him that before he is going to accuse me of anything he should get his facts straight and make sure they were weighing him the same way every day. I insisted that they weigh him again, this time without his diaper. He weighed the same as on the previous day.

He had twenty-two cavities by the time he was two and a half years old. As soon as his teeth erupted, they decayed. The dentist lectured me on tooth brushing every time I brought him in. He had no idea of the tooth brushing skirmishes occurring nightly in our home. On some level, I knew that tooth brushing was not the issue; something was wrong with his teeth. On the other hand, being his mother, I felt responsible, guilty as charged.

These experiences of judgment were difficult because of my own insecurities as a mom. It was so easy to blame myself for his problems and think that maybe if Mikey had a more competent mother, he would be healthier and stronger and sick less often. I believed for so many years that if I had provided a more stimulating environment, he would have developed more normally. If I had loved him better, he would not be so insecure and clinging when in public. I believed that if I had been a good mother, he would have been a happy child.

It was dangerous being a nurse with a little medical knowledge and many nursing and medical textbooks. He had so many varied diagnoses attached to him when he was a baby. In my desperation for an answer or understanding, I would rush home and look up the new diagnosis in one of the textbooks. No matter how far-fetched or dire the diagnosis, I would be convinced that *this* indeed was what he had. This was the answer that explained everything. Eventually, I learned that so many of the diagnoses that I worried about were unfounded. Someone could write an entire book about the affect of a diagnosis on a person. My usual pattern was to latch on to the diagnosis thinking, *"Finally, here is the explanation."* Other times, when it was something I could not handle or didn't like, I would block it out and react with anger.

One time during a hospitalization for pneumonia, they performed a CT scan of Mikey's head. That evening, the resident came into the hospital room and reported to me that the CT scan showed brain atrophy. This means that his brain was smaller than it should be, with ominous implications. I did not want to hear that my beautiful baby had brain atrophy. I became furious at this resident, feeling that he had no business telling me that. I was prepared to deal with the heart, lung, immune, endocrine, and muscle problems that had surfaced so far in my baby's life, but I couldn't handle the thought of something being wrong with his brain. I reasoned, "If the brain is healthy, a person can overcome almost anything else."

I remember finding a pay phone and calling Mike's pediatrician to give him an earful of how bad this resident was. I wanted to kill the messenger. Perhaps the problem wasn't just my anger and denial. The messenger had delivered the results coldly and clinically, without any comprehension of the implications and meaning they had for my son's life in particular and our family's life in general. A "low white blood count" or findings of "pneumonia on a chest x-ray" are common and treatable diagnostic results. A diagnosis of "brain atrophy" is in an entirely different realm. At this point in medical science, there is no treatment for brain atrophy. The resident should have known and understood that.

How could there be anything wrong with his brain?

Occasionally, Mikey was hospitalized in the hospital where I worked. Because I knew many of the people and the system in general, there was a sense of comfort and control over the situation that the average patient does not have. The friends I worked with would visit. I knew many of the ancillary personnel who would pop their heads in the room and tell me how cute Mikey was. That didn't make hospitalizations easy though. My son and I were still "just patients," still at the mercy of the nurses, doctors, and residents. I still had to wait hours and hours for a doctor to round, still had to wait all day at his bedside for a discharge order, knowing that the babysitting bill for his older brother was multiplying by the hour.

During one hospitalization, Mikey's hospital roommate was David, a scrawny, twelve-year-old, redheaded dialysis patient. I knew him well. When the nurse ushered Mikey and me to our assigned room, David and I greeted each other with delight. We were friends. He had been on dialysis since he was ten years old. I had held his hand and talked him through the fear as needles were stuck in his arm. I knew his mother. I had listened to stories of his family and played UNO with him as he became accustomed to the dialysis machine three times weekly. He was in the hospital with a bad peritonitis infection. This is an infection of the peritoneal membranes lining the inside of the abdomen. At this point, he had switched from hemodialysis to peritoneal dialysis. Peritonitis is a common complication.

David liked holding Mikey. Even though he was in pain, he liked sitting in the rocking chair and rocking him. In the evenings when Mikey was asleep in his crib and I was resting on a cot next to it, David would tell me his hopes, dreams, and plans for his future. He hoped someday to marry and have a family. My heart broke as I listened; I did not expect any of his hopes or dreams to materialize. I did not expect him to live long. Though he has since died, it delighted my heart repeatedly over the years to see him accomplish many of the desires he had whispered to me in that hospital room. He received a transplant, graduated from college, and had a girlfriend.

I felt privileged to have been his hospital roommate when Mikey was a baby. When he shared his heart with me, my heart opened to hear some of the hopes and dreams and fears of the other patients that I cared for. After Mikey's early hospitalizations, many patients would look at me in surprise and ask, "How did you know I was feeling that?" or "How did you know that I needed that right now?" Sometimes I would shrug my shoulders and smile; other times I would answer quietly, "I have this son..." Because of Mike, I have traveled to places in the heart and understood worlds that I would not have known about if he had not taken me there. I am also able to understand and forgive all sorts of angry and irrational behaviors displayed by patients and their families because I have been there and done them all. I know intimately the fears fueling the behaviors.

TURNING BLUE

Whenever I feel blue, I start breathing again.[8]

L. Frank Baum

As described in the introduction, individuals with 22q.11 Deletion Syndrome may have a variety of issues. For some, the major issue is congenital heart disease; with others, it is speech. For Mikey, it was breathing. Breathing. Breathing has always been the major concern. The first time he stopped breathing was when he was eight months old. It was a grey, frozen, early January morning. I got out of bed prepared for a tedious cabin-fever day with a toddler and a little baby. Mikey woke up fussy, and as I nursed him, he began to cry, but no sound came out. He turned blue, struggling to inhale. I tried giving him artificial respirations but could not get any air in. His skin turned blue-gray, and then he went limp. He had passed out. In panic, I placed him on the carpet and ran to the phone in the kitchen to call 911.

Then I returned and fumbled through CPR. I couldn't find a pulse—but who knows, maybe it was there? How can you see or count anything when your baby is dying? What I did that morning did not even approximate what I had learned and re-learned many times in CPR classes as part of nursing job requirements. The chest compressions were too hard and too many and the head position wrong. Nonetheless, after all my mistakes and fumbling, he gasped and started breathing again. By the time the ambulance arrived, he was breathing easily and had a good pulse. He was flaccid in my arms and very pale though. The paramedics initially brought him to an urgent care center close to our house.

By the time we arrived, he was pink and sleeping in my arms like a normal eight-month-old baby—that is, if you can call a baby who is too small, too floppy, and with a few developmental delays normal. He looked normal for Mikey. I looked like a normal young mother also. But after frantically trying to get my grey and limp infant to breath again, my world had changed. I had ceased being normal. I had become afraid.

Up to that point I admit I had been a little neurotic. I worried and fretted over many things. I worried about doing something in their babyhood that would damage them for life; I worried about evil strangers stealing my sons at the shopping mall. However, that moment, the moment when he looked dead in my arms, was the moment I crossed the threshold from being neurotic to being fearful.

A palpable thread of fear grew and wove itself into the day-to-day fabric of my life and that of our young family. This fear was the certain knowledge that all sorts of calamities were possible, that it was possible to lose someone dearly loved in a minute. It was the knowledge that I had no control whatsoever, either in preventing disaster or assuring a good outcome.

The paradox was that this certain knowledge of life's precariousness and my own powerlessness led me down the path of becoming a control freak. In the ensuing years, I groped repeatedly for the knowledge, the means, and the power to keep Mikey safe, healthy, and alive. I hoped for a power and control that I did not possess. Not only did I not possess this power and control, but I was reluctant to relinquish it to another.

Actually, it was more complicated than that. Even as a budding, fearful control freak, I prayed all the time for faith and trust, seeking light and understanding. It was a tightrope walk, this tension between faith and fear. Since that first ambulance ride, whenever I see an ambulance, or hear sirens, a fleeting fear tugs at my heart, telling me that someone I love is in trouble. It **is** someone that someone loves. In the words of John Donne, "Never send to know for whom the bell tolls; it tolls for thee..."[9]

The Urgent Care nurses told me that when they received the call about a baby "not breathing," they were panic-stricken, because the previous day they had had another baby "not breathing." Apparently, that baby was playing under a Christmas tree, and a piece of a dough ornament broke off and went into the child's mouth and choked him. The mother didn't know the Heimlich maneuver for infants and tried everything she could, including sticking her finger down his throat to try to dislodge the piece. That attempt apparently caused even more damage, for when the ambulance arrived, the airway was swollen shut. The child was cold and dead by the time the ambulance arrived in the ER. The nurses told me they did not think they could handle another baby death so soon—or ever.

Who was that mother? Because of my narrow escape with Mike, I had a hint of her pain. I thought of her often as my children were growing up. She is probably close to my age, perhaps has other children close to the ages of my children. Does she still weep over her baby who died? Did she ever put up a Christmas tree again? Did she stop being afraid? Was she able to forgive herself?

Another ambulance transferred Mike from the urgent care center to a major medical center. By the time he arrived there, he was cooing, gurgling, gnawing on things, and playing normally as if nothing out of the ordinary had happened that morning. His doctor came to the emergency room to examine him.

She smiled at me, "Your son looks fine. You are free to take him home."

"Oh no! I can't take him home after what happened this morning. He needs to be hospitalized."

"But he looks fine to me," she insisted.

"You didn't see him when he stopped breathing," I exclaimed.

"Sometimes babies just breathe really quietly, and it looks like they aren't breathing," she said gently.

"He was blue and limp. I couldn't get any air in him at first. I am not taking him home. I am afraid," I said with tears in my eyes. She sighed and arranged for his admission to the hospital.

As I sat next to his crib in the hospital, I wrote a letter to Mikey through my tears. I told him of my love for him and my fears—that I hoped he lived a long, long time. I could not imagine life without him. If he died, there would be a hole in my life that no person, no other baby could fill.

The next morning, a lab technician came in to draw his blood, and it happened again. Mikey gasped for air once and then fought to breathe until he again turned blue and limp. They called a code, and the emergency resuscitation team arrived. I watched as they worked on him a little bit, giving him oxygen and pumping his chest much more professionally than I had done the day before. As they were getting ready to stick a breathing tube down his throat, he spontaneously gasped for breath. It looked like they were still planning on putting the tube in, so I moved close to his crib and said quietly, "I think you can stop now. He's breathing again."

Around thirty minutes later, when everyone had left the room and Mikey was sleeping, I went into the bathroom to finish combing my hair. It was still wet from the shower I had taken that morning. The nurses sent a social worker in later that day because they thought combing my hair was an aberrant reaction for a mother whose son had just stopped breathing. They did not understand that only then, after someone else besides me had seen him stop breathing, was I able to relax. I was convinced that someone would figure out the problem, and then I would no longer be afraid.

During that hospitalization the doctors diagnosed Mikey as having "palid breath holding spells." The test for this diagnosis required a doctor to press really hard on Mikey's eyeballs while he was attached to an EKG machine. When his heart rate slowed, the diagnosis was sealed.

Palid breath holding is a benign condition in infancy and toddlerhood, where babies hold their breath when they are upset or crying. The doctors gave me a few articles about it, and I was reassured for a few months. They still insisted that all of Mikey's babysitters learn infant CPR. As I lived with the continuing spells and re-read the articles, I became uncomfortable with the disparity between what the articles described and what was actually occurring when he stopped breathing.

One day, while working in the hospital as a nurse, the resident who performed CPR on Mikey in the hospital came up to me and asked me how he was doing. I told him about a recent pneumonia and a collapsed lung. During our discussion, he told me that he thought my son had been misdiagnosed. He felt the problem was more ominous than breath-holding spells. After that conversation, I took Mikey to another children's hospital in the same city for a second opinion.

Over the course of two years and numerous hospitalizations at two major children's medical centers, no one really figured out what was causing these episodes. The diagnoses and theories multiplied. Each hospitalization resulted in more home equipment for use when he stopped breathing. When Mikey was around two years old, his nursery accessories included an oxygen tank, a collection of airways, AMBU bags (for helping him breathe), a suction machine, a nebulizer, and a breathing monitor. It looked more like a mini-emergency room than a nursery.

The chief of the local fire department came to visit after the first few episodes. He wanted to know everything the paramedics needed to know to help Mikey. He told me that all the paramedics on the squad had taken refresher infant CPR classes because of my son. It was a comfort to me. He was a very kind man.

I never figured out how sometimes he would go one or two weeks without an episode and then, at other times, it would happen a few times per week. On rare occasions, it happened twice on the same day. Since it happened with such regularity, and he always started breathing again, I became cavalier about the entire phenomenon; I no longer bothered to call an ambulance. The ambulance ride, subsequent ER stay, and requisite admission would throw an entire week's schedule out of whack. I reasoned that if he were going to die from these episodes, he would have died already.

Once, while a carpenter was working at our house, Mikey stopped breathing. I went through the routines until Mikey started breathing again and then put him in his crib for a nap. I returned to washing the dishes. The carpenter was in shock. He kept asking, "Did he...? Did I see...? Did you just...?"

Those occasions when Mikey stopped breathing had become routine for my husband also. He also acted with nonchalance when getting Mikey breathing again. On the surface, we had adjusted. Life continued rolling along. However, there were some telltale signs revealing the fear simmering underneath. My husband, Art, was in nurse anesthesia school during these years. He did very well in all his courses until he flunked the pediatric rotation. The problem he encountered in the pediatric rotation was putting breathing tubes down babies' throats to keep them breathing during surgery. He could not do it. This action came too close to his daily fear.

Because my husband was in school, I needed to work if we hoped to eat. There were a few times that Mikey stopped breathing while I was at work, and the babysitter called the emergency squad. My heart would always stop for a moment when the secretary would announce that the fire department was on the line, and they needed to speak to me. So perhaps the truth for both Art and me was that things had become routine on the surface, but underneath the surface, there continued to flow a strong undercurrent of fear.

Occasionally, there were times of divine intervention that kept the fear at bay, convincing me that Mike would live, that God had his hand on my son's life. My favorite story is when the angel rescued us in the blizzard. One cold and snowy Saturday morning, when Mikey was close to one year old, he woke up with pneumonia. He was very sick; he had a fever, his skin looked gray, and his chest rattled. When he coughed, I was afraid he might stop breathing; it required so much energy from him. I was scared.

My husband was on call at the hospital with our "good car." I bundled Mikey and his toddling older brother, Ben, into their car seats and took off in the old Plymouth Duster to the hospital. This old jalopy was so decrepit that rust had created a hole the size of an 8x11 piece of paper in the floor, and you could feel a breeze and see the pavement spin past as you drove along. (I did have it covered with some plywood.) The snow was falling furiously, creating whiteouts where I couldn't see the road. There were barely any cars on the road as I crawled along the freeway in the blizzard. Only an idiot would be out on the road that morning. Then the car stalled. I was out of gas. This was before the time of cell phones, and it was miles to the next exit.

I didn't even have time to worry about the boys getting cold, or what I was to do on this deserted highway, because the very next car that came along stopped. The man didn't ask me what was wrong; he just went to the trunk of the car he was driving and pulled out a gas can. There are stories of angels taking on human forms to perform certain tasks, and I believe he was one of them. Here is why. He had no idea how to work the gas can and switch the spout so you can pour the gas. He didn't even know *where* you put gas in a car. I had to show him everything. When the gas can was empty, he very gently told me there was a gas station at the next exit, and then he was gone.

Every time I remember that incident, I smile. Who drives around with a full gas can in the trunk in the middle of a blizzard? Why did he grab it from his trunk before he knew what the problem was? Why didn't he know how to open his own gas can? I always pictured God in the heavenly court assigning this task to some poor angel but neglecting to give this heavenly being the required in-service on how to use a gas can.

The last and final "not breathing" episode occurred when Mikey was around two and a half years old. My husband and Ben were sleeping, and I was watching TV with Mikey on my lap drinking a bottle. He stopped breathing again, but this time none of the routines worked. I could not get him to start breathing again! Frantic, I woke my husband up, and he called the ambulance while I kept working on Mikey. Once they arrived, the paramedics worked for a while, and he finally started gasping for breaths. After he started breathing, Mikey remained stiff as a board; I could not bend his legs or arms to get his sleeper pajamas on. He was rigid the entire ride to the hospital. This time they took him to yet another, closer children's hospital.

Of course, they wanted to admit him, but when they told us that first in the order of tests were blood gases and a spinal tap (blood gases are painful, and a spinal tap entails inserting a large needle in the spine), we elected to take him home. He was, by this time, sleeping and breathing normally in my arms. They still tried to talk us into admitting him and required us to sign an Against Medical Advice (AMA) form. This is a legal document that absolves the hospital of any responsibility should something bad happen because the patient is unwilling or unable to follow the advice of the medical practitioners.

They called his pediatrician and told her that we were refusing admission for Mikey. She must have smiled remembering the time I insisted on admission and she couldn't get rid of me. After talking on the phone with her, the doctor told me that she told them that if I was refusing admission, he probably didn't really need admission.

After signing the AMA form, we wrapped Mikey in a hospital blanket, took him home, and put him to bed. The next morning he was fine, playing normally as if nothing had happened. He never stopped breathing like that again. Ever. Go figure. Not that life was smooth sailing from that point, but at least there was never another need for resuscitation. The medical equipment in his nursery gathered dust. My husband repeated the pediatric rotation in anesthesia school and passed it with excellence this time. For many years, we had that hospital blanket as a souvenir of that last and final episode.

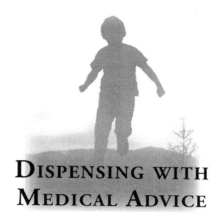

DISPENSING WITH MEDICAL ADVICE

The doctor is often more to be feared than the disease.[10]

French Proverb

That Emergency Room visit was not the first time I refused admission for Mike, believing that I could care for him at home as well or better than he could be cared for in a hospital environment. He already had six hospitalizations during his short life for the apnea spells, pneumonias, and failure to thrive. He had cardiologists, pulmonologists, endocrinologists, neurologists, gastroenterologists, urologists, and allergists at two major medical centers. He had undergone many procedures and tests and had accumulated many diagnoses in the process. I was burned out on hospitals, tests, and doctors. I could not face the thought of more needles, more specialists, more histories and physicals, more lost days in hospitals and doctors' waiting rooms.

In retrospect, I think the main problem with all the specialists was that they only looked at their particular "organ system" when treating Mikey. The neurologist considered neurological diseases; the pulmonologist examined his lungs; the cardiologist evaluated his heart; the endocrinologist considered why he might not be growing as he should; the gastroenterologist did tests on his stomach; the urologist tested his bladder and kidneys. Not one of them asked the question, "What is the meaning of all these odd and varied problems in this one baby? Is it possible that there could be one explanation for everything?"

In previous hospitalizations, I felt guilty for allowing some tests that caused him pain but yielded little useful information. He was not a guinea pig for experiments— he was my son. There was a fear in my heart that the pain and trauma of the hospitalizations, needles, and tests were more damaging to my son's little toddler psyche than the actual disease—whatever it was. Would he stop trusting people? Was he discovering that this life was crazy and unpredictable? Was he learning fear?

There were times I opted out of the recommended treatment like a tracheostomy or human growth hormone.

Other times I *tried* to perform the recommended treatments, but quit them because they were ridiculous or impossible to perform. For example, one time a pulmonologist prescribed Cromolyn aerosols for his asthma. He believed that this medication would stabilize the inflammation in his lungs, decreasing the frequency of pneumonias. It sounded promising, but I doubt his imagination pictured the logistics of trying to keep a mask that was spraying out a noxious substance from a noisy machine on a crying little toddler for fifteen minutes, four times daily. I did attempt to follow the prescription for a week or so, but I quickly concluded that the theoretical benefits were not worth the aggravation. Mikey would be playing happily, and I was going to force a treatment on him that may or may not be beneficial, which would make him cry for fifteen minutes, four times a day? I don't think so. Patients (or their mothers) who don't follow doctor's instructions are classified by the health care community as "noncompliant." I was non-compliant with a capital "N." It was probably easier for me to refuse hospitalizations or dispense with medical treatments because I am a nurse and know how fallible and fraught with complications so many of the tests and treatments for diseases are.

Not only are medical tests and treatments fraught with complications, but the health care system as a whole is often cold and impersonal. Professionals lack compassion and don't listen enough to their patients. For instance, one time when Mikey was a baby, the gastroenterologist wanted to check for reflux, with an esophageal monitoring test. It required a twenty-four-hour hospital stay. The preparation for the test required that Mikey didn't get anything to eat or drink for twelve hours before the test. The test was scheduled in the afternoon because the doctor did surgery and rounds in the morning. I held a crying baby in my arms for seven hours, trying to comfort him, knowing that the only thing that would have comforted him was food. He was hungry, but also angry that I wouldn't give him any food. I hated it. The other problem with being without food for so long was that he was so tiny. He could not afford to go a day without food.

Around five hours after the insertion of the tube, when the gastrointestinal study lab (GI lab) had closed, the connecting wire that was attached to Mikey's chest and the monitoring recorder broke as he moved around. It was a typical run-of-the-mill EKG electrode lead— found all over a hospital.

I asked the nurse if she could find a replacement electrode because I didn't want this test to be wasted. She replied that there was nothing she could do because the GI lab was closed. I asked the interns and residents who were on his case and got the same answer. I asked them to please page the doctor who inserted the esophageal probe, because I was certain that there were a number of extra electrode leads in a drawer somewhere, and I didn't want this day in the hospital to be wasted. Surely, someone could find a lead somewhere to salvage this test! No one was willing to go out of the way to find a replacement lead. It wasn't an important issue for anyone but me.

Around lunchtime the following day, the resident came in to pull the probe, and I asked him to leave it in, explaining that the lead had broken the night before, and nothing had been recorded. I was hoping that even at this late moment, a new lead could be attached and some data obtained from the test. He ignored my request, pulled the probe, and discharged Mikey home.

A few days later, I returned to the gastroenterologist for the follow-up appointment. He said, "I didn't get very much data from this test. It looks like it stopped recording a few hours after the probe was placed."

I responded, "The lead broke off, and none of the nurses or residents on the entire floor were interested in finding a replacement lead. The next day I asked the resident who pulled the probe to replace the electrode and leave the probe in place to get some recordings. He just looked at me, rolled his eyes, and pulled it anyway."

"Well, there isn't enough data from what I have here to make any conclusions. Could you bring your baby in again next week for another try?"

"Not a chance," I replied. "It should have been done right the first time."

"Don't you care about your baby?"

"I do care," I insisted. "It's not fair to put him through another twelve hours without eating. How can you accuse me of not caring about my baby when no one on the hospital ward cared enough to find a simple electrode to spare my son a repeat test? Can't you make any conclusions from the data that you did get?"

"It definitely looks like your baby has a problem with reflux, but I need a full twenty-four-hour monitoring to make that decision. I would like to see what happens at night."

"Don't you think it would be worse at night when he is lying flat, if you were already seeing evidence of reflux with him in an upright position?" I asked him.

"I need a full test to make an accurate diagnosis," he replied.

"I am not bringing him back for another twenty-four-hour ordeal," I replied quietly.

"Well, if you are unwilling to follow through with medical advice and get this test repeated, then there is nothing I can do for your son," he replied matter-of-factly. I left his office, and that was that.

Other times I disregarded medical advice because I didn't like the treatments they were offering my son. The pulmonologist at the second opinion hospital had evaluated Mikey's apnea (not breathing) attacks and had determined that he was obstructing his airway when he stopped breathing. The doctor had identified a large, floppy epiglottis and tracheomalacia (a soft trachea that collapsed). He wanted to put a tracheostomy in Mikey's neck to prevent the respiratory arrests.

As he was describing his plans for the tracheostomy to me, old nursing school videos started running in my head of suctioning green mucus from the hole in his neck and scrubbing little metal cannulas in little silver bowls next to his crib. I wondered how I was going to manage to keep the metal tracheostomy tube tied to his neck with little laces sticky with baby food. I imagined the stoma (tracheostomy hole) getting infected, and pictured his toddler older brother putting peas and corn in the little hole. Mikey was now old enough to make little baby babbling noises and starting to say a word or two; a tracheostomy in his neck would interfere with all of that. Even with the not-breathing spells, I thought of him as healthy. A tracheostomy would turn him into a sick child. I did not want to have my beautiful baby disfigured with a hole in his neck. I listened very attentively to the pulmonologist's plan and description, nodding at the appropriate pauses, and then left his office planning never to return.

Actually, that juncture was the opportune time to start taking Mikey back to the first hospital in town, where he had been diagnosed with palid breath-holding spells. It was a much more palatable diagnosis at that point. I was afraid that if Mikey kept receiving care at the hospital with the pulmonologist recommending the tracheostomy, some other specialists there would read in his chart about the tracheostomy idea, concur, and maybe pressure us into the surgery. There were cases in the news of medical professionals taking parents to court to take them away because they refused chemotherapy for their children.

Even though I was a nurse, (or perhaps it was because I was a nurse), I had many fears about bringing Mikey to the hospital and trusting in the care of medical professionals. One story that sent shivers down my spine was of a mother who had a child with all sorts of weird illnesses at a time when "Munchausen syndrome by proxy" was in vogue in the media. This syndrome is a psychiatric illness in the parent, where a parent purposely makes their child sick. Usually, the parent works in the medical field, often as a nurse like me. Usually, it is a child with a lot of weird and hard-to-diagnose medical problems, like Mikey. Anyway, the zealous medical personnel, delighted in diagnosing their very own case, accused the mother of this syndrome, took the mother to court, and had the child removed from the mother. The child died within a few weeks in the safekeeping of foster parents and hospital personnel.

However, there is always second-guessing about foregoing medical treatment. One never knows for certain if the choices and decisions are the right ones. Mike was fourteen years old when he was diagnosed with Velocardiofacial syndrome (VCFS). This is one of the names for 22q.11 Deletion Syndrome. At that point, I wondered if maybe that one hospitalization at the closer children's hospital the last time he stopped breathing would have led to the diagnosis sooner.

I also ruminated for years about avoiding the tracheostomy. It seemed like an easy no-brainer decision at the time, but as Mike struggled to learn in school, I struggled with guilt. I wondered if those episodes of lack of oxygen had caused some major brain damage, and I was to blame because I couldn't handle the thought of having a tracheostomy hole in his neck.

CHILDHOOD DREAMS

When I bring to you colored toys, my child,
I understand why there is such a play of colors
on clouds, on water,
And why flowers are painted in tint—when I
give colored toys to you, my child.[11]

Rabindranath Tagore

When he was close to the age of three, Mikey's health improved. We believed the worst was over. He was behind his peers developmentally, but he was making progress and developing along his own trajectory. He had settled into a pattern of being around two years behind his peers. My husband and I attributed his delays to being so sick the first two years of his life. We started to believe and hope that Mikey was going to be able to live a normal life. He still remained rather tiny. He was close to a foot shorter than most of his friends in preschool.

Mike playing with a same age preschool buddy.

When Mikey was three years old, his younger brother, David, was born. Our family now had three boys under the age of five. It was a raucous, busy time. Once Davey was old enough to walk and talk, he toddled after his older brothers. He no longer wanted to be in a separate bedroom from his older brothers, so for many years, all our sons shared the largest bedroom in the house. They became a gang of three. They spent their days playing and wrestling like bear cubs.

The Busch boy gang of three. Mike is on the right.

Bedtimes were fun, with all our sons snuggled in their beds as my husband made up stories in the continuing saga of Inky, Spinky, and Dinky, three little boys who spent their days doing crazy things. When the stories were over, it was time for the "soccer tuck." My husband would tightly wrap each boy up in his blanket, relating soccer moves until finally bouncing them on their beds when they made a soccer goal. Once he had finished with one son and moved to the other, the first son would throw off all his covers and squeal, "Again, again! I need another soccer tuck!" After the soccer tucks were finished, my husband and I went to each son's bed, placed our hands on their heads, and prayed for them to grow up strong and good. We believed that God was slowly healing Mikey with our daily prayers for him.

My husband and the boys roughhousing.

When Mikey was a young boy, he had an imaginary friend he called Mr. Nobody, who lived with us and came with us wherever we went. Mr. Nobody frequently did some very mysterious and mischievous things that one would expect of a little boy. Mr. Nobody scattered toys all over our house. Mr. Nobody broke things and just left them there. Mr. Nobody didn't flush the toilet. Mr. Nobody left the back door open and tracked mud into our house.

Mikey carried a blanket with him wherever he went and rubbed it against his cheek for comfort. He craved familiarity and routine. Any little deviation in his schedule would be upsetting to him. When Mikey was around five, he wanted to be Santa Claus when he grew up. He wanted to be the person bringing presents and joy to everyone. He had a gift for seeing things that other people didn't see.

Each spring, he always knew in what trees the birds were nesting and would check on them every day.

He believed that treasures were hidden everywhere and would spend hours digging in the yard to find them. Once, he climbed to the rafters in the old garage, looking for treasures in the old boxes left there by the previous owner. (He fell that time and got a large laceration on his knee.) He loved finding hidden Easter baskets and Christmas presents (which he was not supposed to find). He would spend hours sneaking around, looking for the hiding places. Even though our house had many good nooks, crannies, and secret hiding places, he always discovered the hiding place for the Christmas presents. One year, exasperated with Mikey always finding the Christmas presents before Christmas, I conspired with a neighbor to hide all the presents in her storage shed. Mikey was very depressed the entire month of December as he failed in every attempt to uncover the secret hiding place. He had started believing that there wouldn't be a Christmas celebration that year.

When the boys were little, I taught them to blow the cotton thistle off the dandelion heads and make a wish. Where we live, there are a few days in mid-May when the cottonwood trees release a blizzard of millions of cottony seeds. One day as I drove down the driveway with Mikey in the car, he saw all the feathery puffs floating in the wind. As he got out of the car, he whispered in awe, "Mom, look at all the wishes!" Now, each spring I don't see cottonwood seeds; I see wishes floating in the breeze. So many wishes…

Our county had an early intervention program for developmentally delayed children. A platinum-blond woman named Karen came to our house once a week with a trunk full of toys to help stimulate Mikey's development. Most of the time, the toys bored him. Ben, his pre-school aged older brother, on the other hand, was fascinated with the cool toys and games. He would dance around with delight when her car pulled down the driveway. She would leave a toy or two each week for Mikey to play with, but Ben had the most fun with them.

Even so, Karen was able get Mikey to do things that I could not. One day I remarked to her that Mikey would do things for her that he would have a temper tantrum before doing them for me. She told me she saw this often. She believed he was saying through his tantrums that he needed his mother to be a safe person who would accept him and love him right where he was. It did seem that all through his life others were able to get more performance out of him than I ever could. It took many years to internalize that phenomenon, as I frequently pushed him to the point of tantrums.

The years between the ages of three and twelve were fun years. Mikey would laugh and have fun and snuggle. He loved hugs and kisses. He would wrestle and play with his brothers. He developed friends in the neighborhood, where they would play imaginary games, sports, or cars, and sometimes just run around for hours. Mike loved to be outside running, playing in the dirt, catching lightening bugs, and picking raspberries.

There were so many wonderful moments, so many days filled with laughter and play. We had huge, old blueberry bushes in our backyard. I would send Mike, his brothers, and friends with buckets for picking the berries. They would be gone for an hour and return with just a thin layer of blueberries on the bottom of the buckets. Their hands, faces, and shirts would be stained various shades of blue. Most of the sweet, warm blueberries were in their little tummies. I would have a fit about not having enough berries for a pie, and they would just drop the buckets laughing, and run away to play some more.

Mikey never learned to enjoy board games, puzzles, LEGOs, or building toys. Anything abstract or requiring any visual spatial skill was difficult and consequently not much fun for him. He did enjoy Nintendo and Playstation games, but often became angry when he lost. In frustration at losing, he would start ranting and screaming, "There are cheaters in there!" Sometimes, he would throw the controllers or stomp on them.

He learned his ABCs and learned how to read. To this day, he has yet to learn how to tie his shoes. In his boyhood years, he became fast friends with many of the boys in the neighborhood. Since one of his brothers was twenty-one months older and another three years younger, there were always enough boys in the yard in the general age range to play whatever was the sport of the season. In the spring, they played basketball. Summer was baseball, and fall was football. It was always soccer season. From the time Mike was five, he also played on youth sports teams, mostly baseball and soccer. He was good at sports; the kids liked having him on their team.

Mike in his Little League uniform

Some of the neighborhood boys and our dog Luke

Summer nights were for playing capture the flag after dark. Mike had a "CTF" (capture the flag) mantra that he would start every night after dinner to see if he could call all his friends over to play it when the sun had set. It was a crazy, screaming, noisy time in the dark. They had fun playing sports and hating girls. His best friend across the street would always write stories about him in school and tell his mom that the reason he loved Mike so much was that he was funny and made him laugh. Mike loved making people laugh so he gave up the idea of being Santa Claus when he grew up, and decided to be a comedian instead.

Intermittently during these childhood years, his moodiness started manifesting. He could be happy and jubilant one moment and then, as quickly as a cloud could cover the sun, be in a very dark mood, hating himself—hating living.

Most of the time, Mikey and his brothers got along, but sometimes he would tease his younger brother, Davey, to tears. Other times they would be the best of buddies, playing with their "guys"—about a hundred action figures that they had collected. These action toys provided an escape to a world where boys could be men and do or be whatever they wanted. Mikey would rope Davey into his imaginary games. One game he called "going to Florida." It was a good two-day drive from our house to Florida. We would bundle all the boys up in the station wagon with blankets, games, and goodies for the journey. It is hard to comprehend, but Mikey loved the car ride part more than the actual vacation. He pretended that the upstairs landing in our home was the back of the station wagon. He would pile blankets and toys there and then call for his little brother to come and play "going to Florida" with him.

On one of the trips to Florida, the Busch boys were Teenage Mutant Ninja Turtles

Mike was the one who liked to keep the whole family together and would fret if one person was missing. He was most delighted when he had succeeded in gathering the whole family together in one room. For a number of years we celebrated TGIF (Thank God It's Friday) night. Every Friday, we would get pizza and soda, sit together in front of the TV, and watch the Friday night line-up. Mike loved those Friday evenings more than anyone else.

He loved riding his bike; he would ride it up and down the street and back and forth from his friends' houses. When he rode his bike to the convenient mart a mile or so away with change in his pocket, he wouldn't just buy a snack for himself. He would pick a snack up for each person in the family, and it would be different for each person because he knew what each person loved.

For a few summers, he cared for a guinea pig named Fast as Lightning, or Speedy for short. Speedy was the special education classroom pet. Mikey brought him to live in our home during the summer vacations. He took good care of Speedy; he fed him every day and kept his cage clean. During warm summer days, he would let him out in the morning to run and play in the grass and shrubs, and at dusk he'd scramble around the yard and under and behind bushes to catch him and put him back in his cage for bedtime. Speedy grew sleek and strong, and our other animals—a black Lab and Siamese cat—knew not to bother him because he was Mikey's pet.

The arrangement worked well until one sunny summer day a neighbor's dog thought Speedy would make a nice snack. Our loyal black Lab, Luke, tried to rescue Speedy by chasing the dog down and making him drop Speedy. It was too late. Luke tried to nudge Speedy back to life with his nose ever so gently on the grass. It was a sad burial for Speedy. Mikey had quite a story to tell as he brought the empty cage back to the special-education classroom the following fall.

Mike and Speedy

One of the best summer vacations was when Mikey and the neighborhood boys decided to build a fort in the woods next to our house. All summer long, the sound of hammers banging echoed in the woods from dawn to dusk. They scrounged wood and bricks from wherever they could find them. Whenever we drove anywhere that summer, Mike scoured the roadways for scrap wood. If he spotted some wood, he'd scream delightedly, "Mom, stop the car, stop the car, more wood, more wood!" We also stopped the car for discarded furniture by the roadsides. By the end of the summer, their fort was huge. It had two stories, with at least four rooms on the first floor.

SCHOOL DAZE

I was, on the whole, considerably discouraged by my school days. It was not pleasant to feel oneself so completely outclassed and left behind at the beginning of the race.

Sir Winston Churchill

I hated when I had to go to that other school. It was one of the worst times of my life. The teachers told me I didn't belong in the regular school. I gained a lot of experience with my struggles, but what I want to say is that in the future, I don't want any kid who has a learning disability to be treated like that.

Mike

Since my husband and I had spent so many years in school ourselves, we felt well-prepared for our children to be in school. We didn't realize that having

Mike in school would be the most challenging schooling we had had to date. We were flying blind; blindsided and unprepared for Mikey's difficulties in school. We didn't really forget that when he was an infant a CT scan had showed brain atrophy, but both my husband and I had successfully blocked out and denied that little fact. We reasoned that most people use only a small portion of their brain anyway. Size didn't matter. We had seen him outgrow so many of the health issues of his infancy that we believed that he could overcome almost any difficulty.

Mikey started school in a multi-handicapped kindergarten class, then progressed on to a developmental first grade class, before attending a regular second grade class. In the spring of his second grade year, the school psychologist and other special education teachers decided that he belonged in the special education consortium that a number of smaller school districts had developed to pool their special education dollars for developmentally disabled children. They assured us that Mikey would be happier there and that he would learn better.

The new school in the consortium was a thirty-minute drive from our house. We were uncomfortable with the fact that this alternate school district had a different school calendar with different holidays, different snow days, and different winter and spring breaks than our local school district. Having different days off than his brothers and neighborhood friends created babysitting nightmares. In addition to the babysitting issues, there was also the problem that there was no one to play with when he was on vacation or had a day off. Because we didn't have other options that we knew of at the time for Mike, we reluctantly tried the arrangement.

We encouraged Mike to try to make new friends and make the best of it. One evening, Mike came home happy and excited that he had made a friend at the new school. He showed us the note the friend had given him, and it was stick figures of people having sex. That was the first inkling that maybe this consortium idea was not what we wanted for our son. We didn't know how to address the issue of his strange new friend. Mike didn't even know the child's last name. If it had been a child in our own neighborhood, we probably would have known the parents and known a little about their family. We knew no one at the consortium school. All sorts of crazy thoughts went through our heads about what might be going on at this child's house that he could even draw those stick figures. The unknown is always scarier than the known. We advised Mike that maybe he could find better friends and suggested that he didn't talk to him anymore.

Other educational problems surfaced over the course of that year. I had been reading about special education and the benefits of mainstreaming. The documented benefits of mainstreaming for developmentally and learning disabled children include higher academic achievement, higher self-esteem, and better social skills. In the new school, Mike was cloistered with special needs students who were at multiple grade levels. They didn't do mainstreaming.

I had a meeting with the special education teachers requesting that Mike be mainstreamed for some of the classes. They agreed, but it was a bizarre version of mainstreaming. They would randomly put him in regular classes in the back of the room once or twice a week. He didn't have the benefit of being there every day. Mike told us the teacher would call on him in class and embarrass him in front of the class because he didn't know the answer. That was the only year of his schooling where he made no progress whatsoever. He repeated schoolwork that he had easily mastered in first grade. His teacher told me that he spent his recesses just sitting off in a corner alone.

After trying this unsatisfactory arrangement for a semester, I started the wheels in motion to bring him back to his own district for education the following year. Why ship away the developmentally disabled children? Mike was languishing in this arrangement. It was difficult for him to be away from all his friends and everything familiar. It made much more sense to send the gifted students away—they would have adjusted much more easily. Talk about discrimination!

Arranging to bring Mikey back to the local school was a difficult process. Though this district had special education services for learning disabled children, they didn't provide services for developmentally disabled or physically disabled children. The school district resisted the idea of educating Mikey locally, stating that they didn't have the resources to offer the special education services he needed.

The school administrators did everything within their power to keep him in the consortium. They had specialists observe him in the classroom, reporting that he had adjusted well. I had also observed him in the special education classroom, in the mainstream classroom, and at home and did not share their opinion. The administrators admonished me, stating that the only problem with Mikey in the consortium was my refusal to accept that he was developmentally disabled. It is true that I did have difficulties accepting his disabilities, however the only placement option that they had offered for teaching Mike was woefully deficient. He wasn't happy and he wasn't learning. I also wanted Mike to experience as normal a childhood as possible given his disabilities.

Though the school district was resistant, the law was on Mikey's side. IDEA, the Individual with Disabilities Education Act had been passed two years earlier in October, 1990. One of the provisions of this law states that disabled students have the right to be educated in the least restrictive environment. It was restrictive transporting him thirty miles from his home to a different school district, with a different school calendar from his brothers, and segregating him with other developmentally disabled children.

I learned the law and learned Mikey's rights. I wrote letters and met with school administrators. The school administration stonewalled. A friend of mine who was a special education administrator in another county suggested that I start throwing around the term "due process". He told me it would make the administrators very nervous.

I did not know the steps of due process nor did we have the finances for a lawyer, but I followed his advice, sprinkling the continuing conversations with allusions to "due process." The phrase worked like magic— opening doors like the words "open sesame" opened the treasure cave for Ali Baba in the Arabian Nights. The superintendent finally agreed to educate Mike locally, where he could ride his bike to school, hang around with his neighborhood friends, and be on the same school calendar as his brothers. The plan was to mainstream him with special education support in the learning disabled classroom.

So what happened when Mike attended the local school? Mikey was happy to be back to his old neighborhood school with his friends. It was gratifying to walk through the school halls, pass the kids in the neighborhood we knew, and watch the kids greeting him. The other students accepted him as one of them even with his disabilities. This was where he belonged.

Mike was the first developmentally disabled child educated at the local school district. My advocating for Mike didn't just help him, but made it easier for other children following after him. Once other parents found out about Mike, they asked for and received the same option for their children. There are very few children currently sent away to the consortium, and the special education administrator at the district told me recently that there were plans to phase out the consortium entirely within the next few years.

School itself was still difficult though. He struggled during all of his school years. Homework wasn't a piece of cake either. It was difficult to figure out how to motivate him to get his homework accomplished without doing it myself. Luckily, most of my best artwork looks like a third grader did it.

It took every ounce of energy I had to get him ready for school in the morning. Even if we managed somehow to get him to do some homework in the evening, by morning it was either lost or mysteriously crumpled somewhere in the refrigerator or under a couch. Our dogs really did eat his homework—it was very flavorful with all the food he had dropped on it.

We required that Mikey put his homework in his backpack file when he had finished it. It just didn't stay there. Not only would his homework papers be crumpled or lost, but whatever we had spent time reviewing and learning the night before had also become lost or crumpled in his brain. I loved summer vacation. Other mothers in the neighborhood would bemoan the fact of having the kids home all day. I was just relieved to have a break from the relentless effort required to keep on top of Mike when he was in school.

Mike looking for a homework escape route

It was also difficult for the teachers to figure out how to educate him effectively. To their credit, they bent over backward in an effort to provide him an appropriate education. Individual Educational Planning (IEP) meetings were a nightmare. IEP meetings are official planning meetings for children requiring special education services. These meetings include the child's regular teachers, special education teachers, speech therapist, school psychologist, and a few administrators. The meetings were stressful for me as his mother, because the focus was always on Mike's lacks and deficiencies. I could also tell that the teachers had been pulling their hair out.

Mike had a nonverbal learning disability in addition to his low IQ. This disability means that spelling was easy for him, but reading comprehension was difficult. He could read words, but could not discuss and analyze the meanings behind the words he had read. He could memorize lists and dates, but had great difficulty with visual spatial tasks and terrible struggles with math concepts. He was different from the typical special education student. We really tried to provide the best education for him. We couldn't figure him out. We paid for private educational testing. I enlisted friends who were special education teachers to explain the testing results to me, but they were puzzled by the reports. There were peaks and valleys in the graphs of his abilities. There were some areas that he scored in the normal range in, while other areas very low.

As the IEP group would describe his current struggles, I would smile politely and joke with the teachers, but inside my heart was breaking for my son and his many difficulties. I always cried when driving home from an IEP meeting. I felt so bad for his struggles and so inadequate and powerless in helping him. Once, as I was driving home from an IEP meeting crying, a man talking on a cell phone crashed a red light and smashed into my car. Immediately, a truck driver who witnessed the accident, stopped his truck, ran out, and started yelling at the man who had been talking on his cell phone. It wasn't his fault entirely. I know that if I had not been crying, I would have averted the crash. Driving crying is as dangerous as driving drunk.

When the patrolman arrived on the scene, I was sitting in my car, still crying about the IEP meeting.

"Are you okay? Is anything hurting you? Shall I call an ambulance?" he asked kindly.

"I am fine," I replied through my tears.

"No, really, you should be examined," he insisted.

"I didn't get hurt. Do you want to know what happened?" I asked him.

"I know the whole story already. Before I arrived on the scene, the air waves were buzzing with the story from angry truckers who had witnessed the accident."

He didn't really know whole story. The source of my tears came from a much deeper well than a little traffic accident.

Some days Mike seemed to function much better than other days. He would remember things and be more focused. I tried to figure out the missing magical ingredient. Was it something he had eaten or a missing nutrient? I think mothers are frequently attracted to dietary interventions because it is something somewhat controllable.

There are multitudes of books in print for parents in our situation promising solutions if you follow the simple prescribed disciplinary or dietary steps. I spent hundreds of dollars on books touting "proven" dietary interventions and disciplinary techniques to transform your children's behavior, health, learning ability, or whatever. Today most of these books are gathering dust on the shelves of Goodwill stores. They would do more good buried in the bottom of a landfill somewhere.

We never found anything that really worked. Initially, we were open to suggestions from family, neighbors, teachers, counselors, doctors, psychologists, and friends and tried everything they suggested. However, after many years of hitting brick walls, an exhausted cynicism settled in.

There is now a reference book on the market for parents and teachers of students with a deletion of chromosome twenty-two. It is entitled, *Educating Children with Velo-Cardio-Facial Syndrome*, by Donna Cutler-Landsman. She is a special education specialist, who is also the mother of a child with a deletion of chromosome twenty-two. She published the book a few years after Mike graduated from high school, but I think it would have been very useful in navigating the IEP meetings and planning his education.

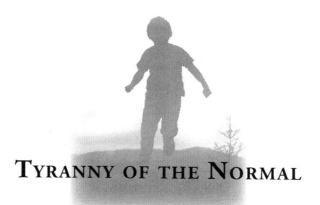

TYRANNY OF THE NORMAL

I hate it when everyone focuses on the problems
I have and doesn't listen to what I have to say. I
am a very sensitive person.

Mike

We kept expecting Mikey to be normal—an
impossible expectation for him. We reasoned
that, "a little better organization, a better disciplinary
system, and things will normalize." Sometimes denial is
good because it buys time to adjust to a difficult situation,
but I think we allowed our denial to persist a few years
past the helpful stage. We used to say that we wanted
him to achieve everything he could, but in retrospect, I
think we were expecting more than he was capable of,
which was cruel. It is hard to know sometimes.

Occasionally, in the course of heart-to-heart
conversations with friends, the question comes up,
"What would you change about your past if that were
possible?" Most of the time when someone asks me

that question, I am at a loss, thinking that one decision changes the entire trajectory of a story. Sometimes unforeseen good things result from bad decisions. To change even a small incident might change the entire story, sort of like Biff and George McFly's relationship in the movie, *Back to the Future.* Nevertheless, there is one thing that I wish I could change. I would have loved him unconditionally, accepted him completely, and enjoyed him just as he was, not expecting him to be normal.

We believed that we were preparing him for life the best way we could by placing normal expectations on him. Isn't that what parents do? Parents teach their children normal behaviors for interacting with the world and succeeding in life. The problem for Mike was that he rarely achieved success in "acting normal." He was so sensitive. I suspect the constant prodding served to discourage him, inculcating a daily sense of failure.

This was a time of many mistakes; of some of them, I am ashamed. Once, when he was struggling to practice the piano, he was having difficulty reading the notes and finding the keys with his fingers. It didn't seem to me he was really trying. I interpreted his frustration as obstinacy. To this day, I remember in shame how in exasperation, as I sat next to him on the piano seat, I shook him. He quit taking piano lessons shortly after that. I am sorry I was so blind.

In an anthology entitled *Tyranny of the Normal,* the editors describe the Greek myth of Procrustes. Procrustes placed all the people who came to his inn onto an iron bed.[12] If they were longer than the bed, he chopped off the overhanging parts; if they were too short, he stretched them until they fit. As Mike's parents during those years, we had some of those Procrustean tendencies in us. Knowing what I know now, especially knowing how sensitive he is, I would have spent a lot less time correcting him, and a lot more time and effort encouraging him, and listening to him. I wouldn't judge his efforts and assume he wasn't trying.

As Mike grew, he stopped liking to be touched. Any physical contact, even to comb his hair or cut his toenails, became noxious stimuli to him. In addition, he did not like music, and if I were playing music in the house or singing, he'd whine until it stopped. (Others in the family might interject at this point that the whining with my singing had nothing to do with Mike's chromosome deletion.) Amusement parks were not fun excursions for him either. The multitude of sights and sounds overwhelmed him, and the rides made him sick. He would respond to the overstimulation either with rage attacks or by retreating into his shell.

We didn't understand these behaviors at the time but have since learned that this is very common with 22q.11 Deletion Syndrome. As most children develop, the sensory system organizes itself around the input the child receives and provides a safe and trustworthy framework for exploring the world. When a child has a disorder in sensory integration like with 22q.11 Deletion Syndrome, the neurological pathways don't develop properly, and the child has difficulty interpreting the various stimuli that assault his senses in daily life. Instead of sensory input providing safe and secure information for navigating reality, the stimuli overwhelm his ability to cope with or interpret it.

It was painful for my husband and me because at the time we did not understand his reactions and interpretations of what appeared to us as normal situations. Over the years, I have learned that Mike reacts with rage when he feels overwhelmed, inadequate, or doesn't understand a situation. When he was younger, I reacted to his outbursts of rage with anger. My response wasn't helpful. I didn't understand the pain and confusion fueling the rage.

During those years, in addition to avoiding touch, Mike also began to avoid eye contact. He misinterpreted social cues in family situations, in school, and other public places. Sometimes our normal looking child would behave inappropriately in public. As his parents, we would feel shame, experiencing judgment from bystanders regarding our parenting skills. For the most part, during those years, his handicaps and disabilities were invisible to the average person on the street. If I could live those years over with the wisdom I have today, I wouldn't have worried at all what others thought about his behavior (or his terrible parent), but I would have been more compassionate toward his socially unacceptable expressions of discomfort and pain, loving him unconditionally.

Mikey's school occupational therapist recommended a therapy to help his nervous system adapt more readily to sensory input. It was called "brushing therapy." With this therapy, the parent or therapist sits next to the child with a soft bristle brush, and gently brushes the child's skin daily, with a firm pressure for ten-fifteen minutes. The theory was that this would help his nervous system develop normal pathways by being stimulated consistently in the same manner.

Though my husband thought it was crazy, I was always willing to try anything that might help. Therefore, for a few weeks, every morning before school I took out this implement of torture—a palm-sized surgical brush with soft bristles. He would scream; he would whine; he would run away. I tried everything to get him to comply with this "therapy," even chasing him around the living room with the brush. His avoidance of eye contact, physical touch, and withdrawing from social interactions are classic warning signs of child abuse. I *felt* like a child abuser those weeks that I attempted to apply brushing therapy. Anyone peering into the window would concur that that is probably what it was.

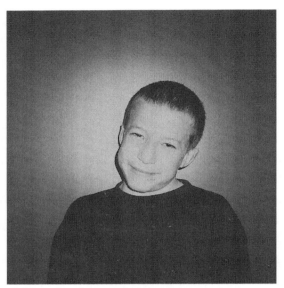

Mike when he wasn't doing homework or
receiving brushing therapy

Some of the current research about 22q.11 Deletion
Syndrome has identified a behavioral phenotype (manifestation of the gene) that often accompanies the genotype (missing piece of DNA). Children with 22q.11
Deletion Syndrome are often emotionally labile, impul-
sive, and display disorganized behaviors. They will
manifest decreased attention, concentration, and display poor social interactions.[13] Overall, they are generally anxious and pessimistic.[14] Each of these adjectives
could describe Mikey during those years.

The discovery that his pessimism and anxiety
had genetic origins blew my mind. In America, the
general conviction is that we can control our destiny,
and even if we cannot control all the circumstances

in our lives, we can at least control our attitude and responses to the circumstances. "Look on the positive side," "hope for the best," and "keep your chin up," are all common admonitions. In my life, I have succeeded in controlling my reactions to a difficult situation by learning to reframe it. We tried to teach this skill to Mike. For years, we read him stories, encouraged him, and attempted to teach and model having a positive attitude. We believed it was a malleable characteristic. I had not considered pessimism a disability similar to blindness or deafness.

Art has a sister who was born with cerebral palsy, and for her, any controlled muscle activity, such as walking or combing her hair, is challenging. It took her years to learn to walk, which she does with difficulty. We would never expect her to be able to play basketball or tennis after a few lessons. The likelihood of Mikey learning a positive attitude from a few stories or behavioral modeling is comparable. It is possible that learning optimism or controlling one's attitude is conceivable for a normal child, but for Mikey and many other children with the 22q.11 Deletion Syndrome, the pessimism is a pervasive, invisible disability with repercussions in all aspects of life.

The question this disability raises is, "Just how free is he?" Where is freedom if you are genetically programmed to expect the worst, to be afraid, or to always see the cup as half-empty? His generalized pessimism was always a challenge for us, and we believed the pessimism is what interfered with much of his motivation to achieve or stick with anything. During a follow-up visit after Mikey's diagnosis with Velocardiofacial Syndrome (VCFS)—one of the names for the 22q.11 Deletion Syndrome—the geneticist asked us about Mikey's motivation. When we described some of the difficulties we had motivating our son, he said that was a consistent theme he'd heard from parents of children with this deletion.

Some psychiatrists nowadays may assert that motivation is a matter for medications. Modulate a neurotransmitter here, modulate another there, and voilà—optimism and motivation are possible! I hope that in the future, psychiatric medications will be that specific and effective. Perhaps, in the future, someone will develop thinking therapies like physical or occupational therapies to ameliorate the invisible disabilities of thinking processes. There is a psychiatrist, Richard Davidson in Madison, Wisconson, who is experimenting with teaching meditation to children with autism and ADHD. What they are finding is that it is possible to change the brain. If only I could motivate Mike to learn to meditate...

NOT ALONE ANYMORE

What kind of God is this? It is a God who increases our capacity to feel the pain of being human, a God who allows deformities and tragedies so we can all be bound together in a sisterhood of need, a brotherhood of desire. [15]

— Fr. Richard Rohr

I really hate this disease. I wish God never created me like this. Why did I deserve something like this? I just feel real bad inside. Sometimes I feel like I have nothing to offer. That's how badly I feel. I just wish I was a normal person.

Mike

Whun Mike was thirteen years old or so, while sitting in a doctor's waiting room, I read an article highlighting stories about people with Williams syndrome. A deletion of chromosome 7 causes Williams syndrome. People with Williams syndrome often have cardiac difficulties, developmental delays, and a low IQ. I read the article and understood that a number of seemingly disconnected health problems could be explained genetically. I knew in my gut that Mike's many and varied problems for which he had seen so many specialists, and received so many diagnoses, had a simple genetic explanation.

There are some similarities between Williams syndrome children and Mike, and for a few months, I believed that maybe this was what he had. However, Mike didn't fit the total picture. He did have the heart defect; developmental disability; short stature; and the long, narrow face, but Williams' syndrome children are generally happy, loquacious, sociable, and outgoing with good eye contact. They have an aptitude for music. Those attributes did not describe my son, but I reasoned that no one ever fits the textbook picture perfectly.

When a psychiatrist wanted to draw some basic blood tests before starting Mike on an antidepressant, I called the genetics clinic at the children's hospital and asked the geneticist what lab tests are performed to check for Williams syndrome. The geneticist laughed.

He asked, "Are you practicing some form of do-it-at-home genetics? What makes you think he has Williams syndrome?"

"Well, I read an article about Williams syndrome and thought he might fit the picture," I replied rather sheepishly. (The geneticist was right; I was performing do-it-yourself genetics with no background or training. I had no idea. What *was* I thinking?)

"What specifically are you seeing in your son that makes you think he has Williams?" he asked.

"Well, he is small, had a heart defect when he was born, and has a mild developmental disability."

"That describes a number of genetic syndromes. Why don't you bring him in for an evaluation?"

"He has been to so many doctors and specialists. Sometimes I worry about what going to all these doctors to find out what is wrong with him is doing to his self-esteem."

"Do not worry. I will be gentle with him. It may be a benefit for him to know the answers to all his puzzling symptoms."

I made the appointment. The geneticist and his assistant took a long and careful health history and then examined Mike. They told me right in the office that they thought the problem was not Williams Syndrome, but Velocardiofacial Syndrome (VCFS), caused by a deletion of chromosome 22. I had been a nurse for over fifteen years and thought that, by this time, I had at least *heard* of most diseases, but this diagnosis was foreign. I didn't like the sound of it.

They told me that they had a mother in the psychiatric ward currently who had also just been diagnosed with the deletion. She had recently given birth to a child with a heart defect and had been so distraught that she attempted suicide. Later, they had tested both the child and the mother, and both were positive for the deletion.

They sent Mike to the lab for a blood test (FISH test) to confirm the diagnosis.

The night that Mike received the provisional diagnosis of Velocardiofacial syndrome (VCFS), I looked it up on the Internet after everyone in the house had gone to sleep. As I read and saw my son described on the various web pages, I *knew* that the FISH test would be positive for a deletion of chromosome twenty-two. It was as if someone had been watching Mike and taking notes his entire life. I sat at that computer until the early morning hours, soaking the information in. I had stumbled into the sunlight after spending a lifetime in a cave.

Oh my God... I thought to myself.

There are hundreds of thousands of children like Mike... hundreds of thousands of parents all over the world struggling with the same issues we are dealing with.

Look at the picture of that kid; he looks just like Mike.

So maybe all his problems aren't my fault. Maybe I am not such a bad mother after all.

Look at that...bad teeth. That explains all his cavities.

Look at the average IQ...that is right in Mike's range. Oh...they call the learning disability a non-verbal learning disability.

That looks just like Mike's cognitive profile. Other parents have troubles with IEPs. I guess a tracheostomy wouldn't have prevented his learning difficulties after all. (To be honest, another reason why I cried after the IEP meetings was that I believed that his learning problems were my fault because I avoided the tracheostomy that the pulmonologist wanted to put in Mike when he was a baby.)

So, it is common for these children to be insecure and moody and to have rage attacks. So, Mike can't really help it. It's part of the syndrome.

So that is why he had all those infections when he was a baby...there is a problem with the thymus. I found a list of one hundred and eighty anomalies sometimes seen in children with VCFS. I spent an hour going through the list and found that of the terms that I understood, my son had seventy-two of the findings.

Up until that evening in front of the computer, it had been so easy to blame myself for his problems, believing that if I had been a better mother, Mike would have been healthy and happy. I saw his difficulties as my fault. What was interesting was that once I let myself off the hook for all his problems, I could be more compassionate toward Mike, seeing and understanding more clearly what he was dealing with.

A friend of mine, a special education teacher, once told me he could not understand why parents frantically searched for a diagnosis for their children with learning disabilities. "Like, what difference does it make? A diagnosis doesn't change anything." That night in front of the computer, reading descriptions about my son on the Internet and reading about other parents' questions and struggles concerning their children changed everything. Not that I had all the answers or could predict the future, but just knowing a little and understanding a little was so much better than crawling around in the dark. There was so much relief in having an explanation or name for the problems. There was the knowledge that I wasn't alone anymore. There were other people out there searching for answers to many of the asked and unasked questions I had been living with Mike's entire life.

The FISH test confirmed the preliminary diagnosis. Where I had experienced relief at the diagnosis, Mike became enraged. The idea of a diagnosis for him was very bad, unwelcome news. When we were driving home after the appointment, I told Mike, "I am going to become an expert on this syndrome, so I can learn everything I can to help you."

"I don't want to have a syndrome. I hate having a syndrome!" he yelled. "Why did you bring me to that stupid doctor? You are always bringing me to stupid doctors! Why doesn't Ben have to go to doctors? I hate you!"

I had been learning slowly over the years not to respond in kind to these outbursts. I drove in silence. After a while, he quieted down and said softly, "I just want to be normal." I understood, remembering my reaction to that resident so many years ago who told me that my adorable, cuddly baby had brain atrophy.

"I'm sorry, Mike. I am not trying to torment you. I love you. I still plan to learn as much as I can to help you. If you ever have any questions about it, just ask me, and I'll tell you what I have learned." It took a few years for him to take me up on that promise, but many times in the ensuing years, he came to me with specific questions about his personality or current struggles, wondering whether it was due to his syndrome. Sometimes the answer was "yes," sometimes the answer was "no", and many times the answer was, "I don't know."

My husband did not share either my relief at the diagnosis or my craving for information. He too just wanted Mike to be "normal." The literature I gave him gathered dust in a pile, unread. For those early years of Mike's life, Art was on the periphery of Mike's issues. He worked full time. I was the mom, working part-time, and the one interacting with the school and the many medical specialists—the one facing daily all the issues and problems. It was easier for him to ignore many of the issues and problems.

We took our family to our first Velocardiofacial Syndrome Conference the summer of 1997. These conferences are combinations of scientific research presentations and parent storytelling. It was comforting to be around other parents who were struggling with some of the same issues we were. In one session, the President of the Velocardiofacial Educational Foundation (VCFSEF) got up to speak.

She looked around at all the parents in the audience and said simply, "You are doing a good job." My eyes filled with tears. No one had ever said that to me as Mike's mom. I knew in my heart that I was doing my best with Mike, even with all the mistakes. However, no one—neither family, nor social workers, nor psychologists, nor doctors, nor teachers, nor neighbors—had ever told me I was doing a good job. I couldn't even say it to myself as I struggled to send Mike off to school neatly dressed, or help him with his schoolwork. I never experienced success as I attempted to motivate him or teach him work and social skills for getting along in this world. Most of the time parents have little need for someone to tell them they are doing a good job. Their children's successes and achievements validate their efforts. It is different with a child with a disability. The efforts are relentless, and the successes rare.

Three things struck me at the conference. First, I recognized and shared with the other parents a raw, visceral hunger to find any possible answers or solutions to the difficulties we all faced as parents. Parents were intense in their attention to the speakers, eyes and ears strained to see and hear every pronouncement. They stood in long lines at the microphone with pointed questions, even when much of the scientific jargon was over their heads. As a nurse, I have attended numerous medical conferences. When professionals attend conferences, there is a vacation attitude, a casual acceptance of the speaker and the slides, a relaxed note taking. Parents, on the other hand, are ravenous seekers of information.

Secondly, I found that I could guess the ages of other parents' children after a brief conversation concerning their current struggles. Parents of infants and toddlers were worried and fearful about the child surviving so many surgeries and health crises. They were exhausted. Parents of children ages three to seven were optimistic, having surmounted so many crises in their child's early years, and now finally the child was doing better. There were a number of children during these years struggling with language difficulties, but the health problems were fewer. Parents of children ages six though twelve were mainly concerned with the learning disabilities and navigating the world of special education and IEPs.

The few parents of teenagers huddled in the corner, sharing psychiatric horror stories and questioning why so little of the conference addressed in a practical manner the psychiatric issues that were so pressing in raising their children. That was an early conference; later conferences have addressed the psychiatric issues. In fact, because of the documented genetic link with the 22q.11 Deletion Syndrome and psychiatric illness, this has been a focus of intense, worldwide research in recent years.

My final observation was that so many of the biological parents of these children had divorced. Some had remarried, so not all were single. Was it the stress of the medical, educational, social, financial, and psychological problems? It is so easy to blame the other spouse when things aren't going right. For many long years, my husband and I were at odds over many issues with no clear and easy answers. We argued a lot. We disagreed on just about everything regarding Mike and his problems.

Another very real stressor is that sometimes the care is all-consuming. The focus is always on the child and his problems, and there is little time or space left for nurturing the marriage. Often the other siblings get neglected. A friend once said to me, "Whenever there is a special needs child in a family, that family is automatically dysfunctional." Probably all families have some dysfunction, but I can assure you we had more than the average dysfunctionality.

We experienced the loss of a "normal" family life. I longed to have a "Leave it to Beaver" dinner hour with everyone neatly dressed and discussing civilly and with humor the issues of the day. Mostly we dealt with irrational outbursts, spilled milk, and very bad table manners. Some days, my husband and I would look at each other from across the table and shake our heads or make faces at each other. Both of us admitted to the envy we experienced when around families with all "normal" children.

Why did we stay together? The glue was the promise we had made so many years before to each other and to God. Contained in the words of that promise is the acknowledgement that every marriage has difficult times, illness, and sorrow. Though discord, arguments, and frustration were our daily bread, the commitment that ran much deeper was the solid floor that kept the bottom from falling out of our marriage. We continued talking and arguing. We prayed and argued and prayed some more and argued and endured.

Was it faith in God that kept us together? Probably. I want to stand before God on my last day and hear him call me "faithful." I also believe that marriage is the best school for learning unconditional love. It is only possible to learn unconditional love when you stick around long enough to face squarely your own brokenness and the brokenness and deficiencies of your partner. There is no limit or boundary to unconditional love. Over the years, we learned that it was not just Mike, but that we are all deficient. Even with a "normal" set of chromosomes, we all lack many things. Learning to give and receive unconditional love is a lesson we all need to learn.

WHAT DO WE DO WITH
WHAT WE KNOW?

Ring the bells that still can ring
Forget your perfect offering
There is a crack, a crack in everything
That's how the light gets in
That's how the light gets in.[16]

                                    Leonard Cohen

P eople inherit two sets of chromosomes: one set from the mother and one from the father. I had read somewhere that in genetic analysis, it is possible to identify whether the deletion happened on the maternal or on the paternal chromosome. Knowing this, one day I asked the genetics professionals whether the deletion came from my husband or me. I was just curious. There is one theory that this deletion occurs in families where there is also bipolar disorder. People with bipolar disorder have a light copy of some of the genes in the q 22.11 region. One theory is this light copy is unstable, and this very instability is the cause of the deletion. Both my husband and I have bipolar relatives. I wondered, "Was it my genes or his?"

The people in the genetic clinic refused to tell us. Did they have the right or responsibility to withhold that information? They probably thought that the question I was really asking was, "Who shall I blame?" They were probably afraid that one spouse would blame the other. I know I would be capable of that in times of irrationality or duress. Would a person blame himself or herself? That happens all the time. I know as a mom I habitually blamed myself over problems my children encountered, problems I had no control over whatsoever. Perhaps when confronted with genetic illnesses, we are tapping into the collective archetypal shame of our humanity. Individually and collectively, we share ideas of perfection and goodness that clash with our obvious and not-so-obvious flaws and brokenness.

At the time of Mike's conception, 22q.11 Deletion Syndrome was unknown. There were no tests for it. Now that we have the technology to identify whether a developing infant possesses the deletion in her mother's womb, what do we do with that information? It is routine in the medical field today to abort defective fetuses.

I am glad the test was not available when I was pregnant with Mike. It would have added an entirely different dimension to the ambivalence of pregnancy. Abortion was never an option for me personally, but I suspect the knowledge that my unborn infant was missing part of a chromosome would have added a layer of fear and taken away some of the joy of being pregnant.

When I was pregnant with my third son, the obstetrician wanted to do some basic testing to identify abnormalities after she heard Mikey's history. I asked her why, telling her that I wouldn't consider abortion. She replied that the possibility of abortion was not the only reason to know. Perhaps other specialists needed to be present when the child was born. Medicine continues to advance so that intricate surgery is successfully performed on developing fetuses. The knowledge that a mother is carrying a defective fetus is a double-edged sword, useful for both life and death decisions. I am hoping that this book will lead prospective parents to choose life, even if it means difficulty and suffering.

There are some bioethical voices that advocate eliminating "defective offspring," even after birth. Peter Singer, a professor of bioethics at Princeton, is a proponent of this belief. In one essay, he used an example of a child born with hemophilia. He said if the child with hemophilia were killed, the parents would most likely have a second child without hemophilia whose life would be better than the first. He wrote, "The loss of a happy life for the first infant is outweighed by the gain of a happier life for the second."[17] He is calculating the value of a human life from a utilitarian, materialistic viewpoint. It is similar to making a choice at the shopping mall, comparing quality and prices between one particular item and another.

What really makes humans happy though? Is it health and perfection? Is he equating happiness with absence of suffering? Is it even possible to prevent suffering on this earth? As humans, we suffer in so many ways. Is suffering the worst evil? It may be that suffering, and learning to comfort someone else who is suffering, is what makes us most human, and teaches us compassion.

Dr. Singer's proposal does not really eliminate suffering, but perhaps substitutes one type of suffering for another. When visiting the United States, Mother Theresa was amazed by the wealth of our material possessions, but dismayed by the poverty of love in our society. She wrote, "The greatest disease in the West today is not TB or leprosy; it is being unwanted, unloved, and uncared for. We can cure physical diseases with medicine, but the only cure for loneliness, despair, and hopelessness is love. There are many in the world who are dying for a piece of bread, but there are many more dying for a little love. The poverty in the West is a different kind of poverty—it is not only a poverty of loneliness but also of spirituality. There's a hunger for love, as there is a hunger for God."[18]

It is easy to believe in the superiority of western civilization because of our technological prowess and the abundance of our material comforts. Perhaps the mark of a truly great society though, is not in advances in technology and materialism but in how it cares for and protects the weak, imperfect, and most vulnerable among it.

Martha Beck, in her book entitled, *Expecting Adam: A True Story of Birth, Rebirth, and Everyday Magic*, describes her experience in the hospital after the amniocentesis had identified that her developing son,

Adam, had Down syndrome. Her physician and the residents caring for her urged her to abort. She declined. Reflecting on the incident later, she wrote, "My real feeling, the one I couldn't articulate yet, was that my entire life hinged on knowing that there were people who would continue to love me unconditionally even if I were damaged, even if I were sick." Her insightful book concludes with, "The lessons I have learned from Adam have hurt more than just about anything else I have felt in my life. And it's been worth it, a thousand times over."[19] I would agree with her in my experiences with Mike. I would not trade this journey for an easier, less painful one. I always carry in my heart the hope that someday Mike also feels that his sufferings have been worth it.

I believe that we are also spiritual beings, beyond our DNA. Our short time walking on this earth is not the beginning, nor is it the end of the story. What we are on this earth is known in part, but what we will be after we die is mystery. Perhaps the major purpose for living on this Earth, with its sufferings and tribulations, is to learn how to love. Maybe in learning to love the "other"—people who are broken, different, and weak— we are learning to love God, the consummate "Other."

I read somewhere that Navaho Indians, when weaving a rug, intentionally weave an imperfection into the corner. It is their belief that this defect is an opening for the Spirit to move into and out of the rug. Perhaps the Navaho Indians are on to something. Could this be the reason why the Master Weaver allows (or creates?)

imperfections in our DNA? Perhaps our human weaknesses and imperfections provide openings for the Spirit to move among us. The blessing of weakness, problems, and needs in others is that they call forth the most love in us, providing opportunities for us to learn and practice compassion.

Mike's life, with all his suffering and struggles, may serve a greater purpose in the direction of our society than the greatest politician, scientist, or writer. Who knows really? What is great or perfect in our eyes might not really be so. There is no one, not even with normal DNA, that you could really call perfect. We are all flawed. That is okay. If you take a walk in the woods, you will never find a perfect tree. All the trees are blemished—the most beautiful ones beaten up a bit by the elements. Yet amidst the disorder and imperfection, the woods overflow with magnificence and beauty.

Having a child with a deletion of chromosome 22 is a grace and a blessing, even if accompanied by much suffering. Mike changed me in ways I could not have predicted, and perhaps in ways no other experiences could have changed me. Mike kept me from living on the surface. Learning to love Mike taught me compassion for myself and for most other people in my life. He gave me eyes to see the suffering of others. Before Mike, I would gaze upon a person with a disability with a cold sympathy, but now because of Mike, I understand and know a deep compassion. I have also learned compassion for those who suffer with the mysteries of mental illness.

PSYCHIATRISTS

All of us are crazy in one way or the other.

Yiddish Proverb

As he entered adolescence, Mike's emotions became more volatile, always veering toward depression. There were times of uncontrollable anger—rage storms. Occasionally, he ran away in his anger. Once, he ran into the back woods late at night with a knife, and it was only Ben who was able to call to him in the deep darkness and talk him into coming back in the house.

Another time, the police picked him up in a neighboring county, wandering from door to door, asking if he could stay at their house since he did not like ours anymore. We tried everything: taking away privileges, different counselors, diet, behavior modification, grounding, punishment, and of course, yelling a lot. Nothing worked.

From the time he was twelve, I was on a quest to find a counselor or psychiatrist who would help Mike. Art did not share my concerns about his psychiatric condition at this point. He was adamantly opposed to the idea of psychiatric medication for Mike. There is a deep shame in having a child with a mental illness. There is a societal stigma regarding mental illness, but the stigma is not just "out there" in the general society; it is so well inculcated internally that the shame and fear interfere with the person or the parent seeking the treatment that would help the person who is suffering.

It was difficult to find a good psychiatrist. We tried a few random psychiatrists who were within our health insurance network. One reminded us of Uncle Fester of the Addams family, another one Mr. Magoo, and we decided that the third one needed a psychiatrist himself. Grasping at straws, I called the local children's hospital and asked for a referral to a good adolescent psychiatrist. They made an appointment for Mike. At the first appointment, I realized that they were hoping to enroll Mike in a study. I told them then that we weren't interested at all in a study; we were hoping to find someone who would take good care of Mike.

They assured me that these questionnaires and steps were what all the patients went through, and that if we didn't want to be in the study, we could still receive the care. Therefore, we complied and filled out the behavior questionnaires and went to three appointments until we finally met with the psychiatrist. He wasn't interested in taking care of Mike; he was investigating a new antidepressant, Effexor.

My husband, Mike, and I met in his office as he attempted to enroll Mike in the study. The study entailed weekly blood draws, EKGs, and other frequent testing. We stated politely that we were not interested in having him in a study. Our main interest was finding someone who would treat Mike as an individual with the best psychotherapy and medication available. When he heard we were not interested in enrolling Mike in the study, he walked us to the door, closing it behind us. When I exclaimed through the crack in the door that his research assistants had promised us that Mike would get care if we went through the steps, he suggested the yellow pages.

Writing this down now, I am wondering why we didn't complain to the hospital board or the state medical board. I think at the time we were so desperate, and still filled with shame at having a son with a mental illness, that we didn't want to do anything that would draw attention to ourselves.

What complicated the search for a good psychiatrist was that the local Mental Retardation Developmental Disability (MRDD) Board in the county where we live in required all their clients to be on Medicaid to be eligible for any services. While looking for a good psychiatrist, we had also applied for Medicaid for Mike for MRDD eligibility. Once Mike was on Medicaid, we couldn't find any psychiatrists who were willing to see him. Psychiatrists don't make a whole lot to begin with, and the Medicaid reimbursement is paltry. We offered to pay out of pocket until a few psychiatrists' office managers told us that because of Medicaid and insurance laws, what I was proposing was illegal!

Mike continued to be depressed and started drinking and using drugs with his friends. He needed to be on an antidepressant. In retrospect, the family doctor probably would have been willing to prescribe an antidepressant. It never occurred to me to try that angle. I think in my gut I felt that his depression was more complicated than the common-variety adolescent depression. He had been diagnosed with VCFS at this point, and I had spoken with other parents and done some reading about the psychiatric issues that accompany the deletion.

In addition to the underlying biochemical defects, there were many educational and psychosocial factors contributing to his depression. He just wanted to be normal. The gap between himself and his peers had widened since the days when they were just boys playing baseball in the yard. He was aware of this gap, and it caused him pain.

ANTI-CARE

What you see and hear depends a good deal on where you are standing; it also depends on what sort of person you are.

C.S. Lewis

I finally found a local clinic that specialized in the treatment of children with developmental disabilities that also accepted Medicaid. After the first interview, I remember coming home and telling my husband that I thought I finally found a place that understood some of the issues we were dealing with in raising an adolescent with a developmental disability, psychiatric illness, and drug problems. After the routine intake assessments, they assigned a psychiatrist and social worker to work in tandem on Mike's case.

This clinic's philosophy was that children with developmental disabilities are over-medicated, and it is preferable to address most problems with behavioral interventions. I do agree with that approach, but in

Mike's case, it blinded them to the possibility that a medication might be helpful. When I told my husband that this clinic didn't like to put their clients on medication but preferred to deal with the problems behaviorally, he was delighted.

The social worker acted as the gatekeeper (and interpreter) for the psychiatrist. Mike and I saw the social worker weekly. She was the one to decide if Mike needed to see the psychiatrist for medication. In the initial interview, I told her of my concerns about Mike's depression and burgeoning drug use. I was thinking that his drug abuse was an attempt to medicate the underlying depression, and I requested to see the psychiatrist to see if she thought an antidepressant might help.

During the second or third visit, at my insistence, the social worker arranged for us to meet with the psychiatrist. She spent a long time speaking to the psychiatrist, then they brought Mike in, and finally they invited me into the office for a few moments at the end of the hour. I used those moments to request an antidepressant for Mike. They both turned to Mike and asked him if he was depressed. He replied, "No." Then they asked him if he was using drugs. Again he said, "No." And that was that.

I think at that moment they expected me to be convinced as to the errors of my thinking. A rare adolescent will freely disclose his drug abuse problems in front of his mom, a social worker, and a psychiatrist. They never considered drug testing or evaluating further for depression.

They told me that an antidepressant wasn't appropriate for Mike.

I stayed with the clinic for over a year anyway, hopeful that perhaps I would learn some behavioral interventions to make things easier at home. Things were getting out of control with his depression, anger, and rage storms. I didn't know how to deal with his marijuana and other drug use.

Occasionally, I would meet with the social worker after she had seen Mike. We would sit next to each other on a chair in the hall. Our conversations were very predictable. The social worker would ask me how I thought Mike was progressing.

"Well, things still seem pretty much the same. He is isolating himself, not very communicative, not sleeping or eating well. He seems sad and angry most of the time. He is not motivated to study, or do any school work, and is still using marijuana. I still think an antidepressant might help him."

"He hates your guts," she would inform me.

"I suppose it is because I am always checking him for drugs and not letting him go out with his friends that are using," I offered.

"He also blames me for being in special education," I added. (He thought all the IEP meetings were my idea.)

"And he is still angry about being diagnosed with Velocardiofacial syndrome. I don't think he even knows how to deal with that yet."

She interjected, "Your son just really, really, really hates you."

I questioned further, "Do you have any suggestions about how I could approach things differently, or do things differently? Is there a better way to motivate him? Is there any approach that would work to get him off the pot? Maybe some medication would help with his depression?"

"Your son hates you. Did you hear me? Do you understand? He hates you."

Of *course* I heard her. I knew he hated me; he told me every day, sometimes several times a day. Not only that, he was in a rap band with his friends and sang, "I hate my mom," at the top of his lungs. It was quite a hit with his friends. I am not sure to this day why this social worker felt that I needed *this* little fact drummed into me. I was "Gestapo Mom," always checking him for alcohol and drugs, grounding him, and keeping him from his friends. I was enemy number one. Of course he hated me!

The drugs and alcohol scared me because he was so vulnerable. It wasn't just marijuana, but I had also found some other drug paraphernalia, droppers, and needles that frightened me. I had been calling the parents of his friends who I knew were using drugs, to Mike's chagrin, giving him more reasons to hate my guts.

I felt so powerless during those years. I was afraid. Those were the years that the inner control freak blossomed. How do you "let go and let God" when your son is using drugs? I never learned how to do that. I was trying to set limits, requiring homework times, preventing his friends from drinking and using drugs at our house, and insisting on curfews. I remembered hating my own mom when I was an adolescent. The fact that he hated me never changed my love for him.

It all came to a head one evening. He couldn't find friends to go out with. He was more agitated than usual, so I watched him carefully, even as he yelled and argued with me. Close to midnight, he went to bed. As part of the spy-mom-surveillance routine, I checked the computer he had been on for some clues as to his agitation. I was shocked to find an Internet chat still on the computer screen where he was asking people for suggestions on how to kill himself, and some people gave him suggestions! I ran upstairs to find him in bed with a plastic bag over his head. The bag had some holes in it, so it probably would not have worked, but I freaked, and called an ambulance. A student in his high school had committed suicide in that manner a few months previously.

I did not take the ambulance with him this trip. I didn't even go to the ER. He was in safe hands, and I needed the sleep. I was too tired emotionally and physically. I was angry with him for the suicide attempt. However, staying home and sleeping that night was a mistake. The next day, when I brought clothes to him in the hospital, he was furious with me, angry, yelling. He didn't want clothes; he wanted me to bring him home. I spoke with the nurses and asked to have the doctor call me so I could give him the history.

The psychiatrist never called. I found the doctor's phone number and called his office every day for three days before I finally decided to page him, and he answered the page.

"I am glad you called back. Mike has been in the hospital for three days so far," I told him on the phone. "We've been trying to get a hold of you," I continued. "Have you gotten the messages that we left? Don't you want to know the story, his medical history?"

He responded, "We were keeping him here for observation, not sure if he is safe at home with you. The nurses reported that he got angry and agitated when you brought him the clothes."

"He was angry because he didn't want to be there. He wanted to come home."

"The social worker at the clinic reports that he hates you."

We never met this psychiatrist. He refused to meet with us and wasn't interested in anything we had to say or contribute. I assume he got all his information from the social worker and psychiatrist at the developmental disability clinic. Months later, after reading his file at the clinic, I learned that they blamed me for his psychiatric issues.

Even though the psychiatrist refused to speak with us, he discharged Mike the following day because the health insurance plan only allowed a few days for psychiatric admissions. The allotted time was up, and no more money would be forthcoming from the insurance company. (He must not have been *that* concerned about my "bad mothering skills.") The psychiatrist discharged him on an antidepressant with a plan to follow up with the developmental disability clinic. Incidentally, Mike's urine on admission was positive for marijuana.

Once Mike was back home, I called the clinic to make a follow-up appointment. The social worker and psychiatrist who had been caring for Mike refused to see him because of the positive urine drug test, insisting that he go to a drug rehab program. They told me they weren't equipped to deal with drug problems.

Why didn't they tell me that when I first brought Mike to the clinic? He had been receiving "treatment" from the social worker for almost a year for his drug problems and depression. For a few weeks, I spent many days dragging Mike to prospective local alcohol and drug rehab programs, but after many long afternoons in waiting rooms and many intake interviews, the story was always the same. They deemed Mike unsuitable for their programs because of his developmental disability. Another difficulty was that Mike lacked the motivation to engage in the programs.

Mike had been home from the hospital for close to a month with only a few days left of his supply of antidepressant, and I still had not found any psychiatric follow up. I had spent hours flipping through the yellow pages, calling one psychiatrist, one agency after another. Either the psychiatrist was not taking new patients, or they wouldn't take Medicaid, or they didn't care for individuals with developmental disabilities.

One cold grey afternoon, after spending a futile day on the phone, calling one agency after another, one psychiatrist after another, I sat at the kitchen table and cried. As I was crying, the phone rang. It was the social worker from the clinic. I was not sure why she called; perhaps she was experiencing some guilt at dumping a patient in crisis.

"Hi, I just called to see how you and Michael were doing," she said in her perky voice.

"I have spent days on the phone trying to find psychiatric follow up for him, and many hours in the waiting rooms of every single drug and alcohol rehab facility in Northeast Ohio. They all do an hour intake and then decide that he is not appropriate for any of their programs." I replied dully through my tears. "He is almost at the end of his Celexa (antidepressant) prescription, and there are no refills, and I still haven't found psychiatric follow up."

"I understand. I have a daughter with cerebral palsy, and I know how difficult it is sometimes to arrange care for a loved one," she replied soothingly.

"No, you don't. You have no idea," I retorted.

"My daughter has special needs. I have arranged physical therapy for my daughter, and have lots of doctor's appointments," she insisted.

"You don't have a clue," I said harshly. "I went to your clinic for over a year," I continued, "hoping that you could help my son. You did nothing for him; you and your silly psychiatrist just spent the time judging and analyzing me. Now, you refuse to see him because it turns out that he *really* was depressed, and he *really* was using drugs. I don't know how you could have been so shocked at his positive urine for marijuana on admission. I have been telling you for over a year that he is using."

"I understand your frustration," she replied sweetly.

Usually I try, though not always successfully, to be polite when I disagree with someone. That day I did not even try. I was so frustrated at not being able to find any follow-up care and so angry concerning the anti-care that they had given my son. I distinctly remember screaming through my tears into the mouthpiece, "You do not understand anything! Do not pretend to understand when you don't! You know nothing. Do not pretend to care when you don't give a shit!" Then, I slammed the receiver down. I never spoke with her again. I suspect that that final phone call confirmed all her preconceived judgments of me.

Because of the extreme difficulty finding follow-up care for Mike, I called the medical director of the clinic and told him of my plight. He assigned another social worker and psychiatrist to follow Mike. It was rather punitive though. I had to drive Mike an hour one way, one day each week for Mike to see a social worker that he really didn't communicate with, just so he could see the psychiatrist and get the antidepressant he needed. This went on for a few long months, until the psychiatrist recommended another psychiatrist he knew who was in private practice and who had an interest in developmental disabilities. We met him, liked him, and transferred our care to him. Mike continued on the antidepressant, and his mood improved. His depression lifted, and he enjoyed his remaining time in high school.

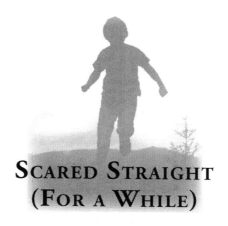

SCARED STRAIGHT
(FOR A WHILE)

I used to smoke marijuana. But I'll tell you something: I would only smoke it in the late evening. Oh, occasionally the early evening, but usually the late evening—or the mid-evening. Just the early evening, mid-evening, and late evening. Occasionally, early afternoon, early mid-afternoon, or perhaps the late-mid-afternoon. Oh, sometimes the early-mid-late-early morning ...But never at dusk. [20]

Steve Martin

We never found a drug rehab program for Mike, but within weeks, police arrested him for possession. A police officer stopped him for a minor traffic violation, and as the officer walked up to his driver's side window, Mike just handed the cop his little stash of marijuana. He arrested Mike on the spot.

We let him sit in the jail as long as we could before taking him home that evening. Art and I went out to dinner and had a few glasses of wine. We were hoping he would get a nice feel for life in jail.

A month later, as the date arrived for Mike to appear in court, I called the police department and asked if I should be doing anything special because of his developmental disability. The officer told me that I should have told them that a long time ago, but now it was too late for him to do anything. He seemed shocked when he learned that I hadn't gotten a lawyer for my son. He suggested I try to speak with the judge.

On the morning of the court date, I made sure Mike was dressed as neatly as possible. I put on a dress. We were both nervous. As I drove Mike to court that morning, I prayed. I was feeling like a bad mom for not arranging things ahead of time for Mike in light of his mental illness and developmental disabilities. I wanted to get him help in quitting pot, but didn't really think that legal difficulties were the solution.

We arrived at the courthouse and found Mike's assigned courtroom. We sat in the courtroom, and as we waited, I watched and prayed for an opportunity to speak alone with the judge. After about an hour and a half, the judge called a recess. This was my chance. I told Mike to stay in the courtroom. (I didn't want him to know that I was trying to speak to the judge.) I quickly followed the judge and his bailiff down a hall and almost followed them right into the men's restroom. I waited outside for the judge to be finished.

As he walked out, straightening out his robe, I accosted him with my anxieties concerning my son.

"My son is in your court room this morning for possession of marijuana. He has a developmental disability. I've been looking for drug rehab programs for him, but he doesn't fit the criteria for any of them," I expanded. "I am not sure what the penalty for his offense is, but I am hoping that somehow you will help me help him. I know I should have contacted you earlier than this morning; I know I should have gotten a lawyer for him…" I rambled on, trying to get the entire story out in the few minutes I had.

"Slow down, relax," he replied when he could get a word in edgewise. "I am glad you let me know. Have you tried Orianna House?" he asked.

I nodded. "Yes, we were there last week. They don't have any programs for him."

He nodded. "I know they will do drug screens," he ruminated.

He added, "This is an area of interest for me. The jails are overcrowded with people with developmental disabilities and mental illnesses. Do not be afraid. I will help your son."

Then I returned to the courtroom and sat next to Mike on a hard metal folding chair for the rest of the morning. His hands trembled, as a trail of unsavory-looking characters wearing orange jumpsuits, flanked on both sides by policemen, hands handcuffed behind their backs, were sentenced to jail terms. He was terrified.

"Mom, what is going to happen to me?"

"Am I going to have to wear those orange outfits?"

"Will they handcuff me?"

"Will I have to go to jail?"

I shrugged my shoulders and answered truthfully, "I have no idea."

Finally, the judge called Mike to the bench. Mike walked to the front of the courtroom and stood before the judge.

"I see that you are charged with possession of marijuana."

"Yes, sir," Mike replied, his eyes looking at the floor, hands trembling.

The judge slammed his gavel on the bench and raised his voice. Mike jumped.

"Don't you know that is illegal? You could ruin your life," the judge growled.

"Do you know what it is like behind bars?" he shouted.

He banged his gavel again, and Mike jumped again. He sentenced Mike to weekly drug screens at Orianna House, for six months. He warned him sternly that if even one were positive, he would go to jail. As Mike moved to the side of the bench to speak to the bailiff, the judge's eyes met my own. He winked, and I smiled. The combination of the morning sitting in the courtroom, his encounter with the "angry" judge, and the requirement for weekly urine drug screens scared him straight for the remainder of high school. It was a tailor-made drug rehab program for someone with his concrete thinking abilities.

THE BEST OF TIMES

Everything has the defects of its virtues.

Old English Saying

Once Mike was in high school, school mainstreaming had a few drawbacks. To paraphrase Dickens, high school for Mike was "the best of times, it was the worst of times. It was the season of hope, the season of despair." Peer pressure is challenging for all adolescents, but much more so when a young person has a developmental disability. The drive to conform and fit in is powerful and intact, but the judgment and decision-making abilities are less developed than those of the average adolescent, which really are not that noteworthy to begin with.

If someone challenged Mike to jump fully clothed into a swimming pool on a chilly evening in autumn, he jumped. A few students took advantage of him. By junior year of high school he had saved up $1000 from birthday presents and jobs, but during that summer he depleted the account in buying pot for himself and his "friends." It was a nightmare.

Yet, high school also provided some very good times. He played safety on the high school football team. Not only was it difficult for him to master the visual spatial task of memorizing the different plays; he couldn't get the football equipment on correctly. No problem though, his teammates helped him. The team wasn't ready until Mike was ready. On those occasions when the coach would put him in for a play or two, they'd cheer him on, chanting, "Mikey! Mikey! Mikey!" As Mike grew and matured he no longer liked to be called Mikey. He preferred to be called Mike. Sometimes though, his friends relapsed and called him his nickname from childhood. They whooped and hollered when he caught an interception.

Mike in his football uniform before a game

Twice the student body voted for him to be a representative on the homecoming court. The school administrators thought that perhaps it was a joke, but I believe the majority of the students cared for him, disability or not, and wanted to include him. The advantage of being mainstreamed most of his life is that his peers already loved him and were friends with him before they were aware of his deficiencies.

Mike riding in the homecoming parade

I have written about the difficulties he had with motivation. The only time in his life where he was 100% motivated was when he got his driver's license. He studied the little Ohio road rule handbook for hours in his room. After flunking the written test twice, they let him take it orally, and he passed. One day, after driving for a while, he found a rubber chicken and duct-taped it to the roof of his old jalopy and drove it to school. His friends found it funny and started bringing in other toys and decorations to decorate his car. Every evening when he came home from school, I would laugh at the funny additions to the menagerie of animals and toys duct-taped to the car. It was a hoot to pass him driving on the road.

Wish I had taken this picture in the daytime

At the high school graduation ceremony, the vale-dictorian praised the class for their giftedness, superior test scores, and achievements as evidence of their great-ness. I sat there thinking, "blah, blah, blah." I knew that the greatness of this class was not in their educational prowess and talents, but in the kindness, friendship, and acceptance that so many students had shown to Mike throughout the years. Mike benefited and continues to benefit from the friends he had in school. I also believe (hope) that his friends benefited from his friendship. In addition to learning English, Math, and Science, they also were learning lessons in patience, acceptance, and compassion. Perhaps that is the most important thing we want our children to take away from school anyway.

During the graduation ceremony, before the principal started handing out the diplomas, he requested in the tradition of all principals in all graduation ceremonies everywhere, that the audience hold all applause until the end. Student bodies in graduation ceremonies everywhere customarily ignore this injunction. When Mike walked across the stage to receive his diploma, the class gave him a standing ovation.

Mike receiving his high school diploma

TRANSITION?

For surely I know the plans I have for you, says the Lord, plans for your welfare and not for harm, to give you a future with hope.

(Jeremiah 29: 11)

It was a typical dinner hour in the summer before Mike's senior year of high school. Everyone was home for dinner. A friend of mine was visiting. The windows were all open, and we were all munching on corn on the cob and barbecued chicken. Mike declared, "I am going to OU (Ohio University) for college, because that is where all my friends are going."

My husband replied, "That is a good school."

My youngest son, Dave, asked, "Who is going to OU?"

Mike listed off the names of some of his friends, "Greg, Jerry, Tom, and Joe."

I said quietly, "Mike, you probably won't be going to college. You don't have the grades or the college prep classes that you need."

He screamed at me, "I hate you! You don't believe in me. You never let me do what I want to do! I want to go to college!"

He got up from the table and ran out of the house, slamming the screen door behind him. My girlfriend took me aside and told me I shouldn't be smashing his dreams like that and that I shouldn't have told him he couldn't go to college in front of everybody. She was right, and I felt terrible.

I wanted him to have hopes and dreams like everyone else. I wanted him to have a future full of hope. However, I didn't know how to have him know that he could still have a future and dreams even if they weren't the same as everyone else's. I wanted him to have hopes and dreams that were realistic and attainable.

In Ohio, special education law provides for the education of someone with learning disabilities through the age of twenty-one. The school district, at this point, could only offer a continuation of the same vocational program that he had hated and refused to engage in the previous four years. That program wasn't an option for Mike.

I had gone to some workshops on "Transition," the new buzzword for having a plan for transitioning special education students from school to adulthood. The main emphasis was "self-determination." The premise is that even if you are cognitively impaired, you are still human and still have the same basic rights of life, liberty, and the pursuit of happiness as every other human. It is a very good premise on which to base services for people with disabilities. The problem is in the implementation.

Where do you draw the line between the individual's desires and what is best for him? Not only what is best for him, but what is possible? It is not only a dilemma for the social services professional, but I encountered it repeatedly as his mother.

I found a program at a local college—the one where I also taught—where students with developmental disabilities from some local districts received job training while working in the college cafeteria. College students who were studying special education were the supervisors. It seemed like a good possibility. Mike loved the idea because some of his friends would be attending college there. During the initial planning stages, his special education caseworker from the local school district seemed supportive. So when all his friends headed to college the fall after graduation, Mike started in the special education work program on the college campus.

It went well for a few weeks, but then Mike started asking if he could live on campus in a dorm with the other college students. It was a long distance for him to drive back and forth from our home every day. It was perhaps because Mike was so insistent on trying it, and visions of self-determination filled my head, that I started looking into the possibilities of this option. I asked around, and the doors opened. The residential authorities said he could live in the dorm, even though he wasn't enrolled as a student. It seemed miraculous that they agreed to that. Mike was delighted to be "going away to college."

He would sleep in his dorm room at night, work in the cafeteria during the day, and eat at the cafeteria with all the other students. He had a work ID badge so he could attend the concerts and other activities on campus along with the other students. I taught on the same campus and could check on him a few times each week. His best friend from high school lived in the dorm next door. I found a microwave oven and other things he could use in a dorm at a garage sale for a fraction of the dollars that it would have cost in a store. That was the clincher. A door had opened wide for him to live in a dorm.

I just wanted his hopes and dreams to come true. We moved him into his own dorm room one fall weekend. He was so happy. (Actually, he was a bit too happy, but we didn't know what to make of it. Most of his life he had been on the depressed side.) We were thrilled to see him so happy. After we had gotten him all settled in his dorm room, he thanked us but wanted us to leave so he could be on his own. We were so hopeful.

When my husband picked him up to bring him home the following weekend, he noticed that Mike's dorm room was a mess and helped him organize it a bit. That weekend, I noticed that Mike didn't sleep that much and seemed more agitated than usual, though agitation wasn't anything really new or abnormal for him.

The following Tuesday we got a call from the cafeteria supervisors stating that he wasn't staying on task. I took him out to lunch on Wednesday. It was a sunny early October afternoon. Mike seemed a little agitated, but not anything different from what I had seen before.

"How are things going for you here?" I asked, as he wolfed down the onion rings.

"I am so happy to be here," he replied, looking directly into my eyes.

"Are you sleeping well?"

"Well, sometimes I just get up and walk around campus when I can't sleep," he offered.

"How is the food in the cafeteria?"

"I like it, but can I buy a few snacks at the grocery store to keep in my room?" he asked. "Sometimes the cafeteria is closed when I am hungry."

"Are there any problems at all? Do you see your friend Eric? Have you made any friends in the cafeteria?" I had a litany of questions.

"I see Eric sometimes, but he has to study. Sometimes I get lonely. I want to have a girlfriend. I also messed up my laundry."

"Maybe we can hire another student to help you with your laundry and with keeping your room clean. Many college students would jump at that chance to earn a little extra cash."

Then I brought up the main subject, the purpose for the lunch.

"We received a phone call from Mr. P. in dining services. He told us there were some problems. You are wandering off and not working at the station where you should be." I was probing, trying to figure out if this was just his usual lack of motivation and poor work habits, or if something else was occurring.

"I like the job. I'll try to do my best," he replied simply. I took him grocery shopping and then stopped by his dorm to pick up his dirty laundry. I told him we'd put some flyers up to see if we could find a college student who needed some extra spending money, who would help him with his laundry and with cleaning his room. I encouraged him to do his very best at work every day. As we said good-bye, he looked into my eyes, hugged me, thanked me for helping him get into the dorm, and told me he loved me. These were all very unusual, very uncharacteristic behaviors for him. However, I loved it, thinking that we were on the right track. I went home, did his laundry, and worked on some flyers to post around campus to hire other student to help him with his organizational skills.

That night at 3:00 am, the phone rang. It was campus security. Mike had tried to kiss a girl in his dorm who he did not know, and she had called security. When they spoke with Mike, they realized that he wasn't making any sense. He thought the police were following him (they were at that point), the TV was talking to him, he was famous, and that he had superhuman powers.

My husband drove there in the middle of the night to bring him home. He was met at the entrance of the high-rise dorm by Mike's two resident advisors (RAs). Both were young women, barely twenty. He saw fear in their eyes. It was still early in the fall semester, and this was probably their first major crisis. They rode the elevator together in silence, the only noise being the rattle of the rickety elevator machinery. When they arrived at Mike's room, my husband knocked on the door, saying "Mike, I have come to bring you home."

Mike opened the door a crack. He was agitated and talking bizarrely. It took a while to talk him out of the dorm room and get him into the car for the car ride home. My husband said he had never seen such a mess as he saw in Mike's dorm room. During the ride home, Mike's conversation consisted of football delusions. He said he was the quarterback of the Jacksonville Jaguars and had spoken with Tim Couch (at that time the quarterback of the Cleveland Browns). He said nothing about the misguided kiss. Mike was still agitated when they arrived home. It took a couple of hours to get him calmed down enough to sleep.

The next day he was upset to find himself back home. He put on his work uniform and babbled, "I have to work and quirk, dishes and fishes."

"I am the great late, freight famous."

"Drive me away. I need to go, to go back jack to the flap jack plack."

I tried to get him to eat something, but he didn't have an appetite. He replied, "Eggs scramble birds, bacon fries oak trees." He continued to spew out nonsense.

"Houses and horses swim under bananas."

"Police pigs picked my pants past the poopy patch."

I drove him to the psychiatrist's office. As I drove, he pelted me with nonsensical words and phrases. Words spewed out of his mouth nonstop. There were more words coming out of his mouth than he had ever strung together in his life previously, but none of them made any sense. The only words he said that made any sense were, "You're cruisin' for a bruisin'." He said this as he tried to steer the car off the freeway. Those times when he stopped breathing as a baby were kindergarten play compared to seeing him in the midst of psychosis.

Once the psychiatrist saw him, he arranged for a direct admission to the psychiatric ward. My husband met me in the psychiatrist's office and agreed to drive him the few miles to the hospital because the ride down had been so scary for me. He had a similar harrowing ride driving Mike in his car. He was afraid that Mike was going to jump out of the car, and wondered how he'd get him through the admission process without Mike running away. He succeeded though. Once admitted, the doctor put Mike on large doses of antipsychotic medication to settle him down. Within hours, he was well-sedated and fell asleep. It took only a day or two before he was talking normally again.

Since that episode, I have read parent stories that frequently children with 22q.11 Deletion Syndrome experience their first psychotic break from reality when away from home the first time. I wish I had known. Perhaps I would have been more protective, not so interested in helping him achieve his dreams. It is hard to say. He had also been smoking pot again, and there are some reports that marijuana can precipitate psychosis in people with 22q.11 Deletion Syndrome.

After the episode of psychosis, the college work skills program refused to take him back. The crash and burn of the college campus adventure was painful. I still worked at the same college, still drove past his former dorm on the way to teach class. It was months before I was able to drive past his dorm without weeping.

Were we crazy to try this dorm-living experiment? Did we try it because we continued to be in denial of his disabilities? I think by this time, we had passed the denial stage. We were aware of his limitations. We expected problems. We were accustomed to troubles and difficulties and had become comfortable bumbling our way through them. It is just that the possibility of psychosis for Mike had not occurred to us. The psychosis was a shock. We were not prepared for it, even after reading articles about schizophrenia in people with VCFS, even after talking with other parents at conferences whose children had become psychotic. It was still shocking and appalling when it happened to our son.

Recently I asked Dave, Mike's younger brother, what he remembered about Mike's episode of psychosis. "Not much," he replied, "I tried to forget it right away.

It wasn't him. He was just sick." In the first draft of this book, I skipped over the psychotic episode, for fear Mike would be embarrassed. There is such a stigma to mental illness. If a person breaks a leg, we can easily separate the broken leg from the person. It is just a broken leg; the person is still the same person. With mental illness, it is a little more difficult to make that clean separation between the illness and the person suffering from it. We quickly associate "crazy" with the person.

After a few days in the psychiatric ward, Mike was discharged home with a new diagnosis: bipolar disorder. He was now on an anti-psychotic medication in addition to the antidepressant. He was over-medicated and sedated. He spent most of his days that fall drifting in and out of a fog as the psychiatrist gradually cut back on his medications. Even though he was sedated, he had returned to his right mind, and we were grateful. He was better, but the loss of the job on campus and the dream of going away to college were major disappointments for him to bear. He had a job for a short time in the local supermarket bagging groceries, but he didn't smile at the customers like the manager wanted him to do. Sadly, they fired him after only a few weeks.

Another search began for a good learning/working/growing situation for him. His caseworker from the Mental Retardation Developmental Disability Board (MRDD) took me on a tour of a number of sheltered workshops for people with developmental disabilities. I do not know if he thought I would think they were acceptable placements for my son, but they were horrible. There would be fifteen or so clients housed in chilly warehouse-like settings with dim lights and no windows. They each had little, repetitive jobs to do, like sorting things into baskets. It was depressing and made me so sad. This was not the future full of hope I envisioned for my son. We looked and looked and looked.

The caseworker finally found the Cadet program, an on-the-job training program for students with developmental disabilities in our county. We got on a waiting list and waited a few months for a slot to open. One of the work options was another college eatery like the one he had worked at, but at a different university.

This was a better learning situation. He had a job coach, and the cafeteria managers were engaged in helping young people with disabilities, sometimes hiring them as real employees after they had worked there for a while. Mike didn't really like the job much though. He would get very anxious each day before work, and throw up in the car as I drove him there. The good parts about this job were that he received a paycheck and again it was on a college campus, so he could still see some of the friends he had gone to high school with.

In June, when the semester had ended, there was a graduation program for the students in the Cadet program. There were videos of the students working, and the job coaches would stand up and describe just what each person did best and how much they had improved over the past year. It was such a happy occasion, so much clapping and so many smiles. There was much love shown to each of the students. As we were driving home that evening, my husband remarked that he had always wondered what the kingdom of God really was or meant. He said, "Tonight, I was sitting in the midst of it." Mike continued in the Cadet program, working in the college cafeteria for the remainder of the summer.

JUST A BROKEN TOOTH,
OR SO I THOUGHT

Life is about not knowing, having to change,
taking the moment and making the best of it,
without knowing what's going to happen next.[21]

Gilda Radner

My parents wanted me to wait a year before I
went to school but I couldn't wait to get there.
I wanted to go so badly. I would do anything to
go there, so I made an agreement that my production at work would be 100 percent because
my production wasn't very good until the end of
the summer. I wanted to prove to everyone that
I could do it. The school was called the PACE
program in Chicago. It was a very expensive
school. I forget how much it cost, but it cost a
lot of money. I know that it was a hell of a lot
of money.

The day finally came when I was ready for Chicago. I can't tell you how excited I was to finally get out of my house. I was ready to move on with my life. I just wanted to be just like everyone else who was going to school.

It was a six hour drive to get there. I didn't say a word to my folks the whole ride there until we got there. Then my mom started to cry. I got nervous and said, "Quit mom, you're embarrassing me." When we finally got to the school, there was a sign-in sheet in the lobby to check in to my dorm room. Man, I couldn't wait for my parents to finish helping me unpack because I wanted them to leave.

Mike

During the months Mike was working in the Cadet Program, he still spoke of going away to school like his friends. In our quest to help him become independent and fulfill his dreams, we spent weekends investigating a few "college-like" programs for people with learning and developmental disabilities. These programs, often based on a college campus, continue basic education while at the same time teaching social and living skills. The goal is for the students to graduate with the skills needed to live and work independently.

One such program is the PACE program in Chicago. We went a few times to look at it, and were very impressed.

Mike completed the application (with my help) and interviewed with the program director and school psychologist. He was accepted. I told the administrators about Mike's episode of psychosis the previous fall and his history of depression, and their response to me was, "That doesn't scare us." They had many students with psychiatric issues. I was beginning to learn that psychiatric issues are part of the territory of developmental and learning disabilities. They had a psychologist on staff who would be monitoring Mike closely.

My best friend from high school lived in Chicago, and a few weeks before school was to start, I discovered my old college roommate was moving to Chicago within walking distance of the PACE program. Again, it seemed like things were falling into place perfectly. There were people he knew, and that we knew and trusted, who could check on him and be there quickly if a crisis developed. It was another hopeful, new beginning. Mike was excited to be going and we worked hard to get everything in order. He did not want a backpack like most high school and college students. He wanted a briefcase. So we bought him one and he put all his important things in it.

Mike can't wait for his parents to leave...

The PACE program was good. They knew how to capitalize on his strengths while preparing him for independence. When we went up there in mid-semester for parents' weekend, Mike gave a PowerPoint presentation to the other students and their families about what it was like to be in the PACE program. We were delighted to sit in on the first parent-teacher conference for Mike where they only had positive things to say about him.

Mike giving his PowerPoint presentation to other students and their families

The first few months there, he did not call home that much and seemed to be adjusting well. Then one Sunday afternoon in November, he called home from his friend's house, where he always went for Sunday dinner. He told us he broke a tooth. On that Monday, the psychologist in the program took him to a dentist where he got an estimate of $1000.00 to repair the tooth. We decided to wait until he came home for Thanksgiving break to have his tooth fixed because it wasn't causing him any pain. He had broken teeth before.

I liked it there. I was learning to be more independent. I was learning how to budget my money, and do my own laundry. I was doing well until my friends got angry with me. They were going to have a big party on Friday. In my meeting with the psychologist he asked me what I was going to do for the weekend and I told him we were going to a party. He told us that we weren't allowed to go. My friend got angry with me, and said, "You ratted us out." I just broke down. I am a very sensitive person. I hate it when people get mad at me. I mean I am a very nice guy. I treat people the way I want to be treated. I hate it when my friends get mad at me. I felt so bad that I just didn't care about anything anymore. Everything just broke down. I just wanted to die. I asked someone for a gun. That's how badly I was feeling.

I didn't want to do anything anymore. I didn't care about anything anymore. I used to lie in bed all the time. I didn't want to go to class anymore. That's why I started calling my mom twenty times a day. I got very depressed. I just wanted to go home. I called my mom and said I was dying. Well, my plan was to go home and kill myself. By coming home I felt like the worst failure.

Mike

We didn't think that much about it at first, but then he started calling, telling us his room smelled, and then he started calling more and more frequently until it was every day and then more than once a day. In the phone calls, he sounded more and more homesick, then anxious, then frantic, and then he started becoming paranoid. We were talking every day with the psychologist and other staff there. Initially Mike had seemed to be holding his own, attending class and his work internship, but when he started staying in his room one weekend and then skipped work on a Monday in late November, I flew to Chicago on Tuesday to bring him home.

When I arrived, he was just sitting in his dorm room on his bed. His room was in disarray, and full Styrofoam food containers were scattered around untouched. The staff had brought food to his room because things had gotten to the point that he wouldn't even leave his room to go to the cafeteria to eat. (His room *did* smell.) He was nervous and sat on his bed as I packed his clothes to go home. Then, we left. The school psychologist and Mike's student helper walked us to the door. We said a casual good-bye with the thought that it would only be a week or so; thinking that Mike needed a minor medication adjustment and then he would return to school after Thanksgiving.

However, he was very scared and walked very slowly, following me at a distance. He was still carrying his briefcase. Previously, I had seen him depressed, seen him manic, and seen him psychotic. But this paranoia was new, and I did not quite know how to approach it. We arrived at the airport and got in the line for the security checks. When it was Mike's turn, the guard said that Mike had a ticket that required the "special security check," and he was required to go down two long hallways to the separate special security checkpoint.

(They let me go with him—thank God!) I am not sure if special treatment for the security check was random, or if his nervousness attracted the attention of the Transportation Security Administration Authorities. It may have also been the briefcase. The shoe removal, wanding, and patting down were terrifying to him. His entire body trembled. Who could have devised a more diabolical scenario for someone in the throes of paranoia?

WINTER OF DESPAIR

Not knowing when the dawn will come I open
every door.[22]

Emily Dickinson

Once I got home, I just wanted to lie on the
couch. My dad was so disappointed in me, he
would say, "Get the hell off the couch." I got
real emotional in my mind from my dad yelling
at me. When people yell at me, I don't talk
to them. My dad kept yelling at me and my
brother David started to cry.

When winter came, I became more and more
depressed. My friends, used to try to get me off
the couch and I wanted nothing to do with them.
I didn't want them to see me like this. I wish I
could have told them what was going on in my
life. I just didn't know how. I didn't want to tell
them the truth that I was planning to kill myself.

Mike

It may have been the choice of medication adjustments or perhaps the sense of failure that Mike experienced at being home again, but his depression and paranoia deepened as the winter days darkened.

The first medication the psychiatrist tried was Lamictal, which was supposed to be a good mood stabilizer, in addition to having anti-anxiety and anti-depressive effects. It sounded perfect for Mike's current psychiatric state. The psychiatrist started the medication slowly, because a life-threatening rash can develop with rapid escalation of the dosage. It was supposed to take six to eight weeks to reach a level to produce a therapeutic effect. He didn't start him on an antidepressant at that point, because antidepressants in someone who is bipolar can precipitate a manic reaction. We gave him the medication and waited and hoped and prayed and watched. Mike wouldn't leave the house. He was terrified if a repairperson or someone he did not know came over. To get him to walk in the yard or go to a movie required herculean effort.

During the first week or so at home, I took him to the dentist to repair his broken tooth. The dentist prescribed him a tranquilizer prior to the procedure. Afterward, when Mike got into the car, he was entirely normal for a few hours, carrying on a normal conversation. He told me how much better he felt with his tooth repaired. I called his psychiatrist, thinking, *Eureka!* Perhaps this spontaneous remission was attributable to the dental work pre-medication. He prescribed the same medication for him to take at home, but that small window of normalcy only lasted that day. By the following day, he had returned to his depressed, paranoid state, and no tranquilizer, mood stabilizer, or amount of love and prodding relieved the symptoms.

Over the next four weeks as we waited for the medication to start working, his condition deteriorated. He wouldn't shower, and he lay on the couch all day. He wasn't even interested in watching TV. Sometimes he would lie there, purposelessly moving one hand back and forth in front of his face. By Christmas, he wasn't even interested in opening a present. If a gift was placed on his lap, he'd maybe rip open one side and then just sit there, not even interested in finding out what was in the package.

The psychiatrist tried other medications. One seemed to help right away, but it made him stiff; another medication caused seizure (one more ambulance ride and lengthy ER stay). Another medication worsened his inertia and stupor. Some days were better than other days. Sometimes, it seemed that he was getting a little better, and we'd be optimistic at the least spark of interest in his friends or the world around him. The psychiatrist started talking about different diagnoses for Mike, such as schizophrenia or schizoaffective disorder.

When I was in nursing school, the major emphasis during the psychiatric rotation was the development of a therapeutic relationship. (In those days, a psychiatric admission lasted three to four weeks, and a therapeutic relationship was conceivable.) We would all gag at these assignments called "process recordings." We were to write out as best we could remember or confabulate, the conversations we had with our patients. The purpose of those tedious assignments was to teach nursing students techniques for drawing out the sick person, to help them feel comfortable and safe. This would help in the development of a therapeutic relationship, and that relationship helped to heal a person gripped by mental illness. Implicit in this approach was the idea that you could talk someone out of his or her psychosis or depression. The concept is wonderful, comforting, and empowering for the psychiatric nurse, but false. It is easier to talk someone out of appendicitis or cancer than to talk someone out of depression or psychosis.

Because my husband and I were products of nursing education in the 1970s, we were so careful regarding our word choices and communications with Mike, thinking that it mattered. It is true that words are powerful, and the choice of words does matter very much in day-to-day relationships among healthy people. However, the problem with a person who is psychotic is that words are impotent, superfluous, just noise. Speaking with Mike those days was like trying to carry on a phone conversation with a busy signal or perhaps attempting to speak long distance to someone using a phone with a severed cord. No matter how carefully chosen, no matter how lovingly spoken, words failed to reach him or help him.

He was admitted to the hospital in late January for starting little fires on the carpet when he was home alone. We felt that he needed hospitalization, that he was not safe at home alone. When I told him we were going to the hospital, he started to get very angry and agitated. I called the ambulance, remembering the other time he was psychotic and tried to steer the car off the freeway. I had been there, done that, and did not want to do it again.

This time the paramedics arrived to our house with police officers in tow, and he cooperated quietly. Once in the ER, it was an all-day wait as he went through the certification process for admission to a psychiatric ward. A social worker came and interviewed him. I begged her to keep him there. Apparently starting little carpet fires is not an approved reason to admit a person into the hospital. In addition to that little insurance problem, the psychiatrist who was on my husband's health insurance plan worked at a different hospital than the one the insurance plan would pay for him to be admitted to. The social worker agreed to admit him, but he was admitted to a hospital with a psychiatrist who didn't know him.

With all the illnesses and health care he had received in his life, I had always found the psychiatric care to be the most difficult to obtain, and the most difficult to endure. Even in this enlightened day and age, with Mike's psychiatric illnesses, I was often implicated as part of the problem. Health professionals rarely blamed me for his physical illnesses, except perhaps the condition of his teeth, and we never had to jump through hoops and approval processes to obtain care. There is enough stigma in our society surrounding psychiatric illness. Why add the humiliation of requiring the patient's family to beg for admission?

Recent health care parity laws now forbid health insurance companies from discriminating against people afflicted with mental illness. I hope that things are improving. The stigma persists though and is even perpetrated by hospitals. If someone is a patient in a hospital with a regular "medical" health problem, it is easy to call "patient information" and get the floor, room number, and condition of the person. If a person has a psychiatric illness, the patient-information people withhold all information, refusing to acknowledge that the person is even at that hospital. What kind of message does that secrecy give to the general public?

Though we made a valiant effort to get him admitted, that admission only lasted two days. During those two days, he didn't shower or interact with any other patients on the ward. The psychiatrist changed a medication and discharged him precipitously. The hospitalization lasted long enough to stress him (and us) out, but not long enough for him to improve. It takes weeks to tell if a medication is working, and the insurance companies aren't willing to pay to insure its effectiveness.

This problem with inadequate hospitalization wouldn't be so bad if adequate psychiatric home care existed. There is none. If a patient is mentally ill and unsafe, and the hospital won't keep them, what does the family do? I spent days trying to get him into a day-care psychiatric rehab program, but the waiting lists were interminable, and he didn't qualify for most programs because of his developmental disability. That winter, my husband and I wrestled with our schedules so that one of us could be home to watch and care for Mike. It was difficult but possible, mostly because both of us are nurses and have flexible schedules. What do people do who do not have the kind of jobs we have?

Not only was it difficult to find good psychiatric care either in or out of the hospital, it was also difficult to share our family's struggles over his psychiatric condition with friends and family. It is a lonely path for families living with mental illness. If Mike were physically ill, people would inquire about his appetite, fevers, strength, and pain—the basic physical symptoms we all discuss and compare when there is a virus going around. With a physical illness, neighbors share many home remedies across the fence with each other. Psychiatric illness, on the other hand, is a strange and scary world. It does not get better with chicken soup or cool washrags on the forehead.

I don't think very many people, except perhaps psychiatrists or psychiatric nurses, would feel comfortable calling and asking about Mike's delusions or ideations. "Is he hearing voices today?" "Were you able to get him to take a shower?" "Is he still digging a hole in the wall of his bedroom?" "Is he still having delusions of President Bush spying on him?" (This was after the Patriot Act. In mental illness, a delusion is a belief held with strong conviction despite superior evidence to the contrary. My husband and I would banter back and forth whether the belief that President Bush was spying on him could technically be classified a true delusion.) It was difficult to fit into a casual conversation that Mike thinks the TV is talking to him, or that he lay on the couch all day waving his hand in front of his head, or that he hadn't had a bowel movement for weeks because he was afraid of polluting the world.

Some days were stranger than fiction. It was easier not to say anything except to the psychiatrist. We didn't know how to talk with Mike and comfort him. As we waited for the medications to start working, I would give him back rubs and feed him healthy meals. He had regressed to needing to be tucked in again at bedtime as he had when he was a little child. It wasn't a "soccer tuck" though. I would cover him so gently, praying with my whole heart that God would cover him with his wings and heal him.

To look at him from the outside, he didn't appear as ill as he was. Sometimes, when a person is in the throes of psychiatric illness, it is obvious from their behavior. They are agitated, wringing their hands, displaying inappropriate emotions, using exaggerated or bizarre gestures, or talking to people who aren't there. They may dress for their own reality and not for the weather. Other times people can be suffering intensely but look and behave entirely normal on the outside.

This happened recently with a friend of mine. She has schizophrenia, and one day I took her shopping at Wal-Mart. She looked good that day and acted entirely normal. We purchased the items she needed, and then I went to get the car so she could smoke a cigarette. As

I drove to pick her up on that breezy, lavender, summer dusk, she looked the picture of peace standing at the entrance to the building, smoking her cigarette. When she got into the car, she told me the aliens in the planes overhead were sending cross beams to her skull. Most of the time unless a person is able to communicate it, what is going on in another person's brain is a complete mystery.

Sometimes, in caring for my son in his mental illness, I found myself starting to act a little crazy. I remember one night, Mike didn't want to take his meds so he tossed them to our puppy, who happily lapped them up. This was around midnight. If I weren't so crazy, I would have just gone to sleep, maybe waking once to check on the puppy. God knows I needed the sleep.

Instead, I freaked out. I became fearful that the medications would kill her, so after spending an inordinate amount of time yelling at Mike, I called a poison control center for animals. (We had had a dog that died suddenly from a car accident, and I didn't want to relive that pain anytime soon.) They advised syrup of ipecac, so I drove about thirty minutes to the only pharmacy that was open for twenty-four hours to be told that it had been taken off the market. So then, I called the animal poison control center back, and they told me to take her to the dog emergency room. By this time it was 2:00 am.

They were quite happy to admit her. They kept her overnight, gave her IV fluids, and charged us four hundred dollars. When I picked her up the next day, I knew that throughout the night our puppy had been fine; happily wagging her tail; never once having any symptoms of any drug overdose. I don't think there was enough of the medication to even affect her. I knew that I had behaved irrationally.

I wondered what Mike now thought about the medicines I was giving him every night. He wasn't overjoyed to be taking them to begin with, but then he watched me become a crazed lunatic when the dog ingested them. The medication seemed to have no effect at all on Mike; I am not sure why I believed it would have such a drastic effect on our puppy.

THE CRUISE FROM HELL

No man needs a vacation so much as the person
who has just had one. [23]

Elbert Hubbard

In the previous fall when Mike seemed to be doing
well in Chicago, my husband and I had arranged
to go on a Caribbean cruise in the spring—just the
two of us. It was not an ordinary cruise, but it offered
the opportunity for a religious retreat entitled, "Catch
the Fire." The Toronto Vineyard, a church in Toronto,
Canada, had been experiencing an outpouring of the
Holy Spirit with many healings, signs, and wonders.
They called this outpouring, "the Toronto blessing."
People from all over the world would pilgrimage to
this church to experience God's love for them in a very
personal way. This experience transformed lives. This
church was the sponsor of the cruise retreat.

When we planned this vacation, I envisioned this
cruise as a time to renew my faith, to get refreshed, and

to soak up the presence of God, along with the sun. Now as the date for the cruise approached, Mike was home with us and very ill. We did not know what to do. We could not leave him at home. There was no one we could ask to stay with him.

So perhaps we were a bit naïve (stupid?), but as we discussed our options, we had the brilliant idea to take him with us along with our other sons. It had been a difficult winter for all of us, and we thought that perhaps a change of scenery, an escape from the winter cold and grayness to the sunny Caribbean, would be better than any hospitalization or medication for Mike. There was also this added benefit of all these holy people praying. Perhaps Mike would encounter God's love and healing. There were speakers on the cruise who had healing ministries. People attending conferences in Toronto reported miraculous healings. We hoped that Mike would find healing there. I hoped for a miracle. I had high expectations and felt blessed to be able to take this vacation.

What were we thinking? Our family still memorializes that lovely Christian cruise as "the cruise from hell." The ship was not a place of healing and rest for Mike. Once on the ship, his psychosis became perilous. He needed constant monitoring because he had this urge to climb the boat railings. We presumed his objective was to jump. He continued to believe that President Bush was out to get him and was terrified to go through any of the passport checkpoints. He attached himself to me, not leaving my side. He became angry and threatening toward his father—acting as if he wanted him dead. It was creepy, this psychotic enactment of the oedipal complex. He was afraid to use the bathrooms on the boat because of fears of polluting the ocean. He wet all the clothes I had packed the first twenty-four hours of the cruise. The only activity he engaged in was putting quarters in the slot machines. There are only so many disposable quarters in this world.

The conference itself was lost to us. I don't remember a single session or teaching because Mike would be sitting next to me—wanting to go somewhere else but there was nowhere to take him (except maybe more slot machines). During the conference, they had "prayer tunnels." People walk between two lines of people who pray for them as they walk or crawl through (sometimes the power from the prayer experienced in these tunnels is so powerful that it is hard to keep standing). Since this was a "Catch the Fire" retreat, these were dubbed "fire tunnels." In the Bible, fire is symbolic of God's presence, love, and purification. My husband and I walked through as many fire tunnels as we could. We were desperate for God's wisdom, presence, love, and power as we walked this journey as parents of a son with mental illness.

The Busch boys disembarking from the cruise. Mike is on the right.

I am not sure how, but moment by moment we survived that hellacious week. As we were disembarking the cruise ship, I noticed other families with loved ones still in their wheelchairs, and realized that we weren't the only ones who had come on this cruise with a hope of healing of some sort. However, we may have been the only ones crazy enough to bring someone psychotic on a cruise.

Shortly after the cruise, the psychiatrist started Mike on an antidepressant. Up until this point, the psychiatrist, in an effort to avoid precipitating a manic episode, had prescribed medications that were either mood stabilizers or antipsychotic medications. Once on the antidepressant, Mike started improving almost immediately. He started to become interested in his environment and interacting with us.

SAINT PATRICK'S DAY

No one ever told me that grief felt so much like fear.[24]

C.S. Lewis

Regardless of how routinely a day begins, there is no way of predicting how it will end. It was St. Patrick's Day. There was still snow on the ground, but the sky was a deep blue, and the icy tree branches were diamonds in the sun. Mike had taken a shower independently (small miracle), and I took him to downtown Cleveland to the international film festival to watch an Irish film. It seemed that Mike enjoyed getting out and seeing all the shamrocks, green hats, and young people playing hooky from school for the St. Patrick's Day parade. We went out to lunch. Things had finally started to turn the corner. He was getting better. Later when we had gotten home, and I had to go on an errand, he did not want to come along. That was a very good sign. He was feeling better, more comfortable being home alone and by himself.

I returned home an hour later in the early spring dusk. A few weeks earlier, my husband and I had signed up for a class on living with a family member with mental illness. This was the third session of the class. My husband had attended the first two on his own, because I had felt the need to stay home with Mike. Now that Mike had turned the corner we planned to attend the class together. The plan was to meet at home, grab a bite to eat, and make sure Mike was settled and comfortable before heading on to the class.

I made it home first, and as I crossed the threshold to the kitchen, I discovered the scene of Mike naked and burned that I described in the first chapter. I called 911 from my cell phone, but they had a difficult time routing the call because I didn't use the land line. It probably only took an extra thirty seconds or so, but it seemed like forever.

As the ambulance whined and careened to the city, I sat in the front seat next to the driver as they stabilized Mike in the back. The young paramedic driving showed me the new technology that controlled the streetlights, giving the ambulance the right of way. He told me that the old fire chief, who had been so kind to Mike when he was a baby, had retired. He also described some other changes in the fire department. My son was in critical condition in the back, and I was carrying on a casual conversation with the driver in the front.

Perhaps that is the typical experience. My personal little life was crashing, but the common life that we all share just keeps tumbling all around, clamoring for attention. It is rather shocking to see how the life all around us just continues to flow, even when we do not think it should or believe it could. A friend of mine's husband needed helicopter transport to a medical center with a ruptured aneurysm. When I spoke with her later, she described the flight as beautiful, the fall colors seen from the tops of the trees exquisite. Since this was only one of many ambulance rides with Mike during his life, the familiarity and routine of it did not prepare me at all for the ordeal ahead.

There are waiting rooms, and then there are waiting rooms. Sometimes when waiting for a person who is seeing a doctor or having a test, waiting rooms can be a welcome respite from the daily routine and a chance to catch up on a book or novel. (Those are waiting room times without a toddler or two to amuse.) It can be interesting watching people in waiting rooms and imagining their stories. This particular waiting room did not fall into any previously experienced categories of waiting rooms.

Outside, the night was dark; inside the lighting was dim. I was alone and very scared, and it was a long, long wait, perched on the edge of eternity. My son's life was in the balance. I thought that my husband was following in the car behind the ambulance, but it seemed to be many long hours before he arrived. He had arrived home when the ambulance and paramedics were with Mike, but waited afterward as the police and firemen spent hours investigating the cause of the fire. They looked into every closet, under every bed, in every drawer. They were aware of his past history of drug use, and I suspect they were looking for a little methamphetamine laboratory hidden in a corner somewhere.

After a very long wait, they let me in for a few minutes to speak with Mike before they put the breathing tube in him. After that he would not be able to talk anymore. He looked at me and told me that he was thirsty and scared. "I am scared too," I responded. He was so vulnerable. I just wished I could take him away somewhere—away from all the fear and pain. I told him that I loved him. It was not possible to decline *this* hospitalization. They sent me back to the waiting room, and my husband finally arrived.

Art and I sat together, waited, and wondered in silence and fear. What was there to say? We had had lots of discord in our marriage, but at this moment we were united in our sorrow and love for our son. We were both in shock. Around midnight, our pastor and his wife came in to sit and pray with us. My friend had called them and told them what had happened to Mike.

An hour or so later, the resident on call came to give us a report. This resident was older, middle aged. He was not a "baby doc," the term used by older nurses to refer to young residents. He was a missionary from Kenya, spending time in the states doing a plastic surgery residency to learn how to repair cleft palates and care for burns.

Over the ensuing weeks as he cared for Mike, we learned more of his story. Bill, the resident, had become a Christian when he was eighteen years old. Though he had been a lackadaisical student in high school, his commitment to Jesus Christ had led him to Hebrew studies in Jerusalem. Once he finished his master's degree at Hebrew University, he seemed to have arrived at a dead end and wondered how he could spend his life serving God.

One day he picked up a hitchhiker on the Gaza strip. The Gaza strip has always been chaotic, but in those days, there were more peaceful interactions between Palestinians and Israelis than currently. As they talked, the hitchhiker told him that he was studying medicine. Bill asked him "Why medicine?" and the young man responded that he hoped to relieve suffering in some small corner of the world in Jesus's name. That one discussion with the hitchhiker changed the course of Bill's life.

From that day on, Bill started the journey to become a doctor. It was a long, tedious journey. He had studied very little science in high school, and none in college. He also was married, and his wife was pregnant. It took many years to get through pre-med while working and supporting a family, and then it took three years of medical school rejections until he was finally accepted. For all those years, they lived and raised a family, which by then included five children, on a salary below the poverty level. He completed medical school and became a general surgeon. The journey to becoming a physician had taken eighteen years!

After finishing medical school and residency, he took a position as a missionary, serving in a village in the remote mountains of Kenya with his family. He loved the people and the deep blue skies in Kenya. Once, when changing Mike's central lines, he described the skies in Kenya as bluer than anywhere else in the entire world. He practiced there in an eighty-bed hospital that sometimes had water—sometimes had electricity—for six years before he decided to return to the states for a plastic surgery residency to help treat the cleft palates and burns he encountered in his daily work. Like the hitchhiker, he had wanted to alleviate suffering in the name of Jesus in some small corner of the world, and here he was taking care of my son in an American city hospital.

The night of the burn, he reported to us that Mike had suffered third and fourth degree burns in over 60 percent of his body. He then told the calculation of how much fluid they would need to give him to keep him alive the first twenty-four hours. He requested permission to perform escharectomies. He explained that as Mike's body started to swell from the burn and the fluid resuscitation, his cooked outer skin would start to act as a pressure suit, cutting off the circulation. If this pressure weren't relieved, he could lose a limb or two. They planned to cut long slits down both his arms and along both sides of his torso to relieve the constriction.

We waited in that dim and silent waiting room as the surgeon performed the surgery. After waiting a few more hours, they said we could come and see him. The nurses oriented us to the procedure we would be following every day as long as Mike was a patient in the burn unit. Before entering the burn unit, there was a washing and gowning room. At a giant sink, we learned to perform a surgical scrub on our hands and arms and then don yellow gowns that covered all our civilian clothes. The purpose of this ritual was to protect all the burn patients on the unit who were so vulnerable to infection.

I am not certain how well this ritual worked to prevent infection, but in the first few weeks, I came to understand the value of this ritual as a community builder for all the families of the burn patients. I imagine it was akin to the community that once existed at the village well, where the women went daily to draw water for their families. As we scrubbed and gowned, we drew water for each other as we discussed our loved ones, their burn accidents, how they were doing—how we were doing. As the weeks went by, we discussed our families, our own lives and struggles, our fears and our fatigue.

When we walked into Mike's hospital room that night, the nurse tried to warn us that Mike would look different. His face had swelled, and there were many IVs and machines. We felt prepared, especially being nurses, thinking that we'd seen everything, but it was a shock to see his head so fat and swollen. His lips protruded like a fish's mouth opening and closing in the water. He was unrecognizable. If someone had asked us at that point to identify his body, we would not have been able to. He was wrapped in gauze dressings from head to toe. There were tubes in his nose, mouth, urethra, and two large IV lines in the big veins in his chest. There were many IV pumps with many liters of fluid attached to those two main lines. There was no place to even touch him or hold his hand.

The nurses tried to prepare us for the coming months. They described the recovery from a severe burn as an interminable roller-coaster ride. They predicted that some days he would look better, and we would leave the unit with hope for his future, and the next day he would crash or develop a fever or infection. They predicted that if everything went smoothly with Mike's 60-percent burn, to expect a two-month hospitalization.

We arrived home from the burn unit close to dawn. The house had that acrid, stale odor of a campfire that has turned cold. There were burn marks on the kitchen cabinets. The hardwood floor had deep, black scars where Mike's clothes had smoldered in piles as he had ripped them off in his mad dash to the shower. The shower curtain was charred and melted. In our tears and pain, we tried to piece together the events as they must have transpired. Was he really cooking meatballs? Or, did he burn himself on purpose?

Stool clogged the upstairs toilet. The past month in his mental illness he had had some delusions about moving his bowels. He was afraid he would pollute the world. In fact, he had become so constipated that he had started vomiting, so that morning before we went to the movie, I had given him a laxative to move his bowels. The laxative must have worked, and then the toilet clogged up. Did that freak him out? Was that what happened? Was it a suicide attempt? Whatever or however it happened, instead of dropping and rolling, he ran. He finally made it to the shower to put the fire out but not soon enough to prevent the third degree burns now covering his lower face, neck, chest, back, arms, and buttocks.

My heart ached to picture Mike on fire—running first to the kitchen sink and then to the shower to try to put out the fire. "My son, my son," I said, weeping. I couldn't stand the picture of him running around in pain with his clothes on fire. I went to bed and slept the black sleep of agony for maybe an hour or so, but my crying woke me up.

> I wanted the fire to kill me. That's how bad I was feeling. Thank God you came home. I didn't know what to do but you saved me. That's no lie. I remember I was in pain, lying naked and I remember I really didn't want to talk to you. I was in so much pain. I remember they gave me morphine and that's all I remember.
>
> Mike

SITTING IN SORROW

Remember always that each person sits next to
their own pool of tears.[25]

Trevor Hudson

T he next morning, still in shock, my husband and
I got up and showered in the bathroom with the
melted shower curtain and fire-stained sink. I wept
to see again the charred scars the fire had made on
our house and floors. Visions of Mike's pain and fear,
running and crying and frantically trying to put out the
fire alone haunted me.

Returning to the hospital and seeing him all
wrapped in gauze from head to toe and with all the
tubes and monitors was again a shock. I felt again that
old maternal, visceral pain of having my insides ripped
apart. The same old familiar pain—only this time it
was so much more intense because his body was so very
damaged. I knew if he lived, his body would never be
the same. In my years as a nurse, I have seen and cared

for many very sick people. It is so very different when the person lying there is your own flesh and blood. Everything hurts, and there is so much fear.

I spent the next few weeks in a blurred vigil at his bedside—mostly crying and in such sorrow. I was usually able to hold one of his hands, but was unable to rub his back or face or show any other physical contact. I could not speak; I could not pray. I was angry with God and hurt by his neglect and silence. Thousands of my prayers alone had been poured out for Mike over the previous twenty-two years—prayers for healing, for hope, for love, for a future full of hope for him. What good were they? I sat next to his ruined body. Machines, IV drips, and tubes kept him alive.

In the past, I had prayed for many things and had some miraculous answers to prayers. However, this *one prayer* for hope and healing for Mike had been lifelong. A deep heart every day, every beat of my heart prayer since the moment I first laid my eyes on him, and this—this was God's answer? I remembered the Catch the Fire cruise a few weeks earlier and the fire tunnels. I complained sarcastically to God. "No, you misunderstood. This is not the fire we were asking for." I also asked him where Mike's guardian angel had been hanging out at the time of the burn. Why bother rescuing a stranded car, but not rescue Mike from burning himself? What were these heavenly angel priorities anyway?

The paradox was that even with all my anger, confusion, disappointment, and sorrow, I knew God as my friend. Over the years, I had grown to love Him and know His presence. I trusted and needed Him. I had always turned to God when my heart was breaking. I fell at His feet weeping, like Mary, Martha's sister, when Lazarus had been dead for four days, accusing God of neglect (John 11:32-33). "If only you had answered even one or two of the prayers I had groaned for Mike over the years, this never would have happened to him. If only You had been here…"

I was quarrelling with my friend at the time I needed him most. Yet, even as I argued with God, in the deep, dark, empty, hollow silence of my own grief, fear, and sorrow, I felt His tender presence alongside me. He suffered with me, suffered with Mike. He suffered with all the other families on the burn unit. He wept as I wept. The omnipotent God who did not answer my prayers, and allowed terrible things to happen to our family was weeping as I was weeping. He held me in his arms as I pounded against his chest. I waited and wept in the dark, empty, silent abyss. I had no words to say. There was nothing left to say or ask for. There was only this deep silence of not knowing anything. The only thing I knew was my broken, shattered heart.

The sorrow was a familiar place. Over the years as Mike's mom, I had come to understand that I was a citizen in this land of sorrow. Sometime in the course of Mike's life, I had read an article about the phenomenon of "chronic sorrow."[26] This describes the chronic, deep pain that parents of disabled or chronically ill children live with. In 1967, Simon Olshansky coined the term to describe the lived experience of parents of a child with a disability. It is often not recognized by the parents themselves or those around the parents—their relatives, friends, and professionals. Chronic sorrow doesn't mean that parents don't love or feel pride in their child. These feelings exist alongside the sadness. The grief is the loss of the expected child, the loss of the normal expectations that parents all have for their children. There are so many losses to grieve.

When Mike was a young child, I grieved with every illness, every hospitalization, every new diagnosis or problem, every developmental milestone that he failed to achieve. When he started school, I grieved with every homework assignment he couldn't accomplish, every low grade on his report card, every IEP meeting. I think this sorrow is not so much a loss of something present, but also the loss of a bright future for his life.

As he grew older, there were different losses, like watching him become the outsider among his peer group. Once, I found myself weeping at a junior-high choral concert. It wasn't the cacophony of adolescent voices that evoked the tears. It was seeing all the friends that he played with when he was younger. They were together laughing and goofing off on the stage, but my son was alone, by himself, on the periphery.

In high school, I watched him struggle to keep up with his peers, wanting to do everything they were doing, and yet, by this point, he wasn't just two years behind his peers' grade level intellectually, but left in the dust socially and emotionally. Commonly, developmentally disabled individuals find younger and younger peer groups as the kids their own age mature. Mike wasn't content with that. He always wanted to be with his same-age peers. It broke my heart to watch him struggle to be normal when day after day he would fall on his face.

There is a quote in the book of Lamentations in the Bible that exclaims, "All you who pass this way, look and see: is any sorrow like the sorrow inflicted on me" (Lamentations 1:12 JB). As I sat there wallowing in my own deep sorrow, I started to understand that my sorrows were not unique; they were just a part of the *one* sorrow that we all share. It just reveals itself in different stories.

On the street where my sons grew up, I could describe the sorrows each home, each family had experienced over the years. There was a family who had a twelve-year-old boy who one day raced his bike down the hill, hit an oncoming car, and was decapitated. (I later cared for his mother when she was one of my dialysis patients.) Three teenage boys lost their lives at the bottom of the same hill a few years later, driving while drinking after a graduation party. In another house, a father died suddenly at age forty, leaving two young sons. On this same street are stories of marital infidelity, incorrigible children, divorce, alcoholism, and financial hardships. A little baby died of cancer. A young mother died of cancer a few months after delivering her little daughter. That is just one small street in an ordinary town in Ohio.

Then there is the world. A few months before Mike's burn, the Indian Ocean tsunami killed two hundred thousand people. While I sat in the burn unit, the death tolls from the wars in Iraq and Afghanistan were mounting daily. There was Darfur. Every day, all over the world people suffer terrible illness, loss of loved ones, wars, and tragedy. Foolishly, we find many reasons to separate us one from another, but sorrow is something we all share.

While sitting at Mike's bedside, I read the story in the book of John about Lazarus. It was close to Easter and Mike now looked like Lazarus after he had died, wrapped in gauze head to toe. As I read and prayed, I heard in my heart the same words Jesus spoke to Mary when she was weeping in his arms, "This sickness will not end in death, but it is for God's glory so that through it the Son of God may be glorified." (John 11:4, JB). I wished for the acceptance of Job, who told his wife after they had lost everything, "If we take happiness from God's hand, must we not take sorrow too?" (Job 2:10, JB).

Not only was I angry with God, but I was riddled with guilt at not being able to communicate my love better to Mike when he was physically well but struggling with depression. I remembered the times he had asked me to rub his back, but I had been too busy, and now I did not know if I would ever get that chance again.

What had I been so busy doing?

What had been so important?

Now I was spending whole days sitting by his bedside waiting, watching, and praying. What if I had spent even a fraction of that time with him before the burn—maybe he would not have felt compelled to do it. I wondered at how I had not seen nor could ever have predicted this happening. I made so many, many mistakes in loving him. There was so much I didn't see or understand.

My nursing knowledge also accused me for not seeing and preventing this tragedy. He had been so depressed before the burn, and the psychiatrist had recently started an antidepressant. It is common knowledge in the medical field that for the first few weeks after starting on an antidepressant the severely depressed person is the most vulnerable, most likely to attempt suicide. The energy is back, but the despair and hopeless feelings are still hanging around. I am his mother—a nurse. Why didn't I see that possibility? Why didn't I protect him?

Earlier that week I had found a bunch of kitchen knives in his bed. Now that is bizarre, and in retrospect should have been a clue as to his suicidal inclinations. The problem is we had become accustomed to bizarre, and he had been digging holes in his bedroom wall for some time. We had told him then that if we found knives in his bed again he would be going back to the hospital. I felt like an idiot for not following through when I had the chance.

Though we threatened hospitalization, we did not really consider psychiatric hospitalization a viable option at that point. We had a history of three useless psychiatric hospitalizations under our belts. There was little hope that another hospitalization would be helpful. We believed that he would do best in the loving, supportive environment of our home, and that my husband and I (two nurses) would be more than adequate to keep him safe and watch for any unusual behavior or changes. So much guilt attended those ruminations at his bedside, so much recrimination.

Here is where being a nurse makes the situation quite murky. The years of training, compulsive re-checking, and over-responsibility somehow duped me into thinking that I had more control than I really did. I believed that, if I did everything right, I could insure a good outcome. Conversely, if I made a mistake, it would always result in an adverse outcome.

Sitting at his bedside with so many hours to ruminate and feel guilty, I started to question how much of a situation is really under my control. I had always wanted to keep him safe and healthy, but even though I studied everything, prayed every day, and did everything within my power to protect him, I had failed miserably. I started acknowledging that I didn't have the control, the wisdom, or prescience that I coveted. The will and desire to help him were always there, but not the power or authority to ensure it.

HOSPITAL STILL LIFE

Hospitals are places that you have to stay in for a long time, even if you are a visitor. Time doesn't seem to pass in the same way in hospitals as it does in other places.[27]

Pedro Almodovar

After the first few weeks or so on the unit, things started settling into a routine. Spending days at his bedside became my day job. I drove to the hospital every morning, parked in the visitors' parking garage, and walked over the bridge to the hospital. I wore a backpack containing my laptop, papers to grade, my cell phone, a book or two, and some snacks. A certain hospital odor, which can only be described as a mixture of cleaning solutions, body secretions, and dressing compounds, greeted me each morning. My husband and I had personalized visitors' badges and parking passes; we learned all the shortcuts and knew where to get the best coffee. We learned the names of the nurses, the housekeeping staff, and the volunteers. We knew the names of the families of George, Martin, Timothy, Brian, Sarah, and Josh, the other burn patients. What broke the routine always was seeing Mike so sick and raw and suffering. That was a daily shock and always brought me to tears.

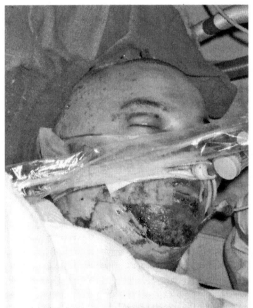

Mike after a few weeks in the burn unit

The days developed a surreal quality. I felt like we were living in a Salvador Dali painting (the one with the wilted clock sliding off the table and the carcasses in the background). One day melted into another. It was easy to forget what day or week it was or what happened when. I forgot appointments and people I had promised to call. The to-do list that had previously constrained my days disappeared. There was nothing to do. Nothing needed to be done. Day-to-day life continued for the rest of the world, but we had fallen off the carousel.

There were the morning blood draws and then the doctors' rounds. Mike's surgeon always told me how good Mike looked, and I would tell him he was a little crazy. After that came the bath. First, they would sedate him more than usual. Then, a team of six or so nurses and techs would put on masks, gowns, and gloves. They worked as a team to remove the dressings and the dead tissue. They would scrub the burned areas and then wrap everything in gauze again. In the past, I had heard stories of burn patients describing the bath as the worst torture of the burn. When they bathed him, I would go to the chapel to pray, but not really praying, as I had previously known prayer. There were no words. I sat in silence, but there was One who sat with me, holding me.

When the bath was completed, Mike would look all fresh and be neatly wrapped in white fluffy gauze from head to toe. That picture of cleanliness lasted only an hour or so before the gauze became a multicolored, soupy mess with the range of wound drainage colors spanning from blood red to browns and yellows to pale green and even to purple from one of the dressings used.

Every week they would take him for another surgery to replace the dead skin with skin grafts taken from the few areas on his body that had normal skin. Sometimes they had to use artificial skin because there wasn't enough normal healthy skin on his legs for them to harvest. They shaved his head and used skin from his scalp to replace the burnt skin on his face, chin, and neck.

They told us that Mike's chances for survival were good because of his youth. However, we knew that the tiny deletion of chromosome 22 would complicate matters. His lack of parathyroid hormone made the calcium levels in his blood erratic. He might be more susceptible to infection because the thymus gland, the master gland in the development of the immune system, is often poorly developed or missing in a person with 22q.11 Deletion Syndrome. This problem with the thymus gland was the reason for so many of the infections he suffered as a child. Even though as he had grown his immune system had become smarter and better able to deal with ordinary infections, we worried about a possible remaining deficiency that would sabotage his recovery.

Another worry was the possibility of bleeding. Often in his life, his supply of platelets was low, causing him to bleed more than the usual person. Once he had had a plantar wart removed from the bottom of his foot and hemorrhaged for hours afterward. Would his low platelets cause him to bleed to death after one of the surgeries?

Within hospitals, there exists a social order with different classes or subcultures. Some examples would be the nursing culture, the medical culture, the administrative culture, and the culture of the housekeeping staff. Each of these subcultures shares a language, similar roles, traditions, and expectations. There are shared jokes and understandings. During those early weeks in the burn unit, my husband and I discovered yet another underground hospital subculture, shared by families of critically ill patients. Initially we knew each other by the visitor's badges, but soon we recognized faces as we saw each other every day. We would bump into each other at the coffee cart, in the cafeteria, and at local eateries. We shared a language of the heart and the eyes. We all had new day jobs at the bedside of our loved ones. We shared hopes, sorrows, and fears. Sometimes we communicated with a nod of the head in passing. Sometimes we cried and hugged each other. Sometimes we laughed. We were part of an elite hospital subculture that no one wanted to join.

People would ask my husband and me if it was easier walking through this because we were health professionals. I never knew the answer to that question. Sometimes our "nurse mode" was a great escape mode. We could focus on the monitors, labs, drips, and respirator settings and forget that it was our son entangled in all this. Other times we would fret over a change in vital signs, a new symptom, or a lab value that a medically naïve parent would not know to worry over.

Throughout those long weeks, our friends, coworkers, neighbors, and church family carried us. They kept us well fed by bringing us meals and taking us out to eat. I discovered that food is one of the currencies of love. We felt so loved and cared for when we would return home from the hospital to home-cooked meals. We knew so many people were praying for Mike and for us. We felt the prayers, certain that they were what gave us the strength to walk through each day. Many friends came to Mike's bedside to pray for him—sometimes when we were there, sometimes when we were at home. Receiving so much love taught me to love better.

Kathy, the younger sister of a friend of ours at church, (well she was not young, she was in her seventies), would come to visit and encourage us. She told us that when she was seven years old, she had crawled into a car and played with matches, and the car caught on fire. She had had 60-percent third-degree burns like Mike, and she told us that all the skin on her hands had burned off. This was in the 1940s. In those days, they didn't have the antibiotics and other marvels of modern medicine that we have today. Her hospitalization had lasted for over a year. How could she have survived? (I did hear stories though of her mother spending the days at her bedside praying.)

Kathy now had children and grandchildren. Her skin looked like the average skin of a seventy year old, a bit loose and wrinkled, but no obvious or disfiguring burn scars. Whenever she would visit, I would stare at her hands as she spoke, watching her use them and marveling at the skin covering every bone and tendon.

THE DREAD NURSE MOTHER

Pain has an element of blank;
It cannot recollect
When it began, or if there were
A day when it was not.[28]

Emily Dickinson

During the end of his second week in the burn unit, Mike started spiking fevers. These were different from the fevers common to burn patients from the high metabolic rate. These fevers were higher, and his whole body would shake as if he were having a seizure. Around the time the fevers were fulminating, the burn team decided it was time to remove his breathing tube and take him off the respirator.

Everyone on the ward was jubilant and delighted at his "quick recovery." Everyone was smiling, except for me. My nursing instincts told me that he was crashing and very ill, and no one else was seeing it. I worried about his fevers. Every time they changed his catheters, they would send the catheter tips to the lab to culture for infection. The results were always bad bacteria (mostly pseudomonas and staph aureus—common hospital-acquired infections that can cause death in many cases), but for some reason, they weren't drawing blood cultures on my son. I asked the nurse who was taking care of him why they weren't taking blood cultures, and he replied that he felt he didn't need them.

"This is just the usual fever we see in burn patients. You need to trust us," the nurse replied.

"When he was on the antibiotics last weekend after the last surgery, he didn't have the fevers and chills that he is now suffering with. And look at his blood pressure—it is too low, and his heart is beating too fast. He has a bad infection. He needs blood cultures. He needs to be on some antibiotics."

"We don't like to give antibiotics; they are not your friend."

"Pseudomonas and staph aureus aren't my friends either," I replied, understanding and knowing from years of nursing experience that antibiotics often cause more problems than they resolve. There is a danger of creating multi-drug resistant bacteria in burn units. Since I understood the dilemma, I requested that an infectious disease specialist come and see him. I knew that my son was in trouble, and I was scared.

Two infectious disease doctors walked in later that day as I was sitting by the bedside. "I am glad you came," I told them. "He is looking sicker to me. I know they have cultured staph aureus and pseudomonas from his catheters. I am worried that he might be getting septic."

They stood at his bedside for less than a moment and gave him a perfunctory look. "We know that you think he needs antibiotics. We don't like to give antibiotics until a person is septic," they said and then walked out.

I sat at my son's bedside and looked at him. His whole body was shaking from the fevers. His blood pressures were very low, and his heart was beating very rapidly. I looked at him and asked myself, *If this isn't a picture of sepsis, what is? How much sicker can he get?*

The only thing good about getting the breathing tube out was that he could speak to us in between trying to catch his breath. The first words out of his mouth were, "I didn't do it on purpose." The nurse at his bedside remarked that comment was a sure sign that he *did* do it on purpose. Frequently, severe burns are suicide attempts. It didn't really matter to me whether it were on purpose or not. At that point, I just wanted him to live. I felt bad that he was afraid that I'd be angry with him.

I spent that night in the hospital at his bedside, for he was getting agitated. They couldn't sedate him as much with the tube out because of the danger of suppressing his respirations. That night was the longest and darkest night of my life. He spiked temperatures up to 105° F, despite a cooling blanket, Tylenol, and Motrin. His respiratory rate was in the range of forty to sixty breaths a minute. (A normal respiratory rate in humans is twelve to sixteen breaths per minute.) He was gasping for air, using every muscle in his chest to get the next breath. His heart was beating up to 180 beats per minute. (A normal heart rate is around 80 beats per minute.) He could not sleep and would moan in delirium. He wasn't making any sense. I sat next to him with my head on his bed, holding his hand, and sharing his agony.

I wondered if ever in my entire nursing career I had seen anyone as sick or suffering as much as he was suffering. His moans, pain, and agonized breathing ripped my insides. The left side of his face drooped, his left eye was cloudy with infection and drainage, his ears were black with pieces falling off, and his neck and face were bloody and raw. He had tubes in his nose, his teeth chattered, and every muscle in his body trembled. The rest of his body was an open sore. Every movement caused him pain. He had a Foley catheter, a rectal catheter, and enough intravenous lines to support fourteen bottles of fluid and medications.

However, even with all the bottles of fluid pouring into his body, he was dehydrated. More fluid was seeping out from the open areas of his body without skin than he was receiving intravenously. His lips and tongue were cracked and dry. He kept moaning how thirsty he was, and the scant amount of urine in his Foley bag was concentrated and very dark. He asked for his shoes.

"What do you need shoes for?" I asked.

"If I have my shoes on, I can go home."

"You can't walk; you can't even stand. I wish I could bring you home, but I can't."

"I could use a scooter, like Aunt Laureen." (Aunt Laureen is Art's sister who has cerebral palsy.)

He begged me to take him home or just let him die. He was so weak he could barely lift his arms or legs. I wished I could take him away from all the pain and suffering, but all I could do was sit there, hold his hand, and say quietly,

"I am here."

"I love you."

"I am so sorry."

The next morning I waited and waited for the weekend doctor on call to come and see Mike. I had a list of concerns. I was hoping they would increase his fluids, again consider antibiotics, and check his chest x-ray. I was concerned about pneumonia with all his difficulty breathing. I was exhausted when my husband arrived in late morning, because I hadn't slept the entire night. The surgeon on call still hadn't made his rounds. I described the night to my husband and then wrote down all the things that I hoped he would mention to the surgeon on call that weekend. I asked my husband and Mike's nurse to tell the doctor everything and went home to sleep.

Later, when I returned to the hospital, the message from the doctor on call, relayed to me by both my husband and the nurse caring for him, was that I should, "be a mom and not a nurse." He ignored all my requests and concerns, changing nothing. A few days previously, I had noticed a corneal ulcer and infection developing in Mike's left eye. I told the nurse. She had replied, "Sometimes patients eyes get gunky."

"That isn't just gunky," I replied. "He's got a bad infection in that eye." I went on sharply, "*If* he survives this burn, he's going to want to be able to see out of that eye." The nurse didn't do anything about it, even after my little outburst, but when Mike's surgeon came in that afternoon, and I showed it to him, he called in an ophthalmologist right away. Mike not only had a bad eye infection, but a corneal ulcer had developed which could cause blindness.

After that incident though, the head nurse came in and told me that I needed to trust the nursing staff more and "just be his mom." It became a recurring theme over the next few days as I struggled to get Mike the attention he needed as he deteriorated. Because I am a nurse and accustomed to the hospital nursing culture, I am familiar with the process of labeling patients and their family members. I imagined the break room conversations, knowing that they had labeled me as an over-worried, controlling, hysterical "nurse mother." The hospital lore is that nurses make the worst patients. It is possible that nurses who are mothers of very sick patients surpass all other classes of dreaded nurse patients.

Labeling patients and family members serves a purpose ,in offering an illusion of understanding and control in the chaos and uncertainty of caring for very sick patients. It may also serve to build a community among the nursing staff in sharing a common understanding. The danger though is that a label can blind a nurse to what is really happening with his/her patient.

When my husband told me the doctor's response to my concerns, I started crying. My husband even believed that I had no business telling the doctor what Mike needed. No one was listening! I knew I had never cared for a burn patient, never worked in ICU, but I did know Mike. He was my son. I had cared for him his entire life and watched him breathe (and not breathe at times). I learned to recognize pneumonia before it became pneumonia and to detect other subtle changes and intervene in time to prevent a health crisis. I knew when he was sick or in trouble, and here I was sitting next to him in the hospital, and he was sicker than I had ever seen him or any other human being. No one would listen and give him the fluids and the antibiotics that he needed to survive. I tried to be diplomatic and patient, believing that keeping a good relationship with those caring for my son would somehow ensure better care for him.

In the days that followed, I berated myself for not making a scene until someone listened. I hadn't trusted my churning gut enough. I had doubted myself, thinking maybe the professionals knew more than me. I had let the desire for keeping a good relationship with the staff muzzle my mouth. How did a good relationship with the staff matter more than my son's life? There are a few steps I could have taken that weekend. I could have called his regular surgeon at home, I believe that he was concerned enough about Mike to come in and see him. I could also have called the hospital ombudsman. My mind wasn't working right at the time.

I was also distressed over the recurrent admonition that I be Mike's mom and not his nurse. I knew that if I were his nurse, I would have known whom to go to or whom to call to get him what he needed. I had advocated successfully for many patients, sometimes saving their lives—but as his mother, I felt impotent. I took issue with the idea that I could ever stop being a nurse and stop seeing things through a nurse's eyes. The only time that a mother could be a mother only and not a nurse would be if she were not a nurse. How could I pretend not to know what I knew, not to see what I saw?

The remainder of that weekend was a downward spiral for Mike. This was *after* I thought it wasn't possible for anyone on this earth to be any sicker. Mike became more and more delirious and confused. He was so thirsty, his mouth and tongue were cracked dry, but every time I tried to give him fluids by mouth, he would vomit. He struggled to breathe, needing to use all his chest muscles. I was terrified.

On Sunday evening when I left, they turned off his tube feedings because he was going to surgery in the morning to graft more skin on. I had a hard time sleeping that night because I had never seen my son— never seen anyone in my whole career as a nurse—as sick as he was. I woke up in the middle of the night in a terror, and since I couldn't get back to sleep, I called the nurse who was taking care of him to see how he was doing. He told me that they had given him Lasix, a diuretic, because his urine output had stopped. I freaked. His urine output had stopped because they had stopped the tube feedings. He was already dehydrated before that. Lasix, under these conditions, had the potential to damage his kidneys. This was a special concern for me being a dialysis nurse. I did not want dialysis to be part of his future. I drove to the hospital at 3:00 a.m. and made them call the doctor, and I had a fit until they gave him a bolus of fluid. Even what they gave him at that point was not enough. I sat there at his bedside until dawn watching him in a death agony. He was cheyne-stoking, a breathing pattern that patients often fall into as they are dying.

Mike *was* dying.

When dawn came, I walked next to his cart as they took him to the operating room. As the anesthesia people took his cart, I told them he was dehydrated and to please give him lots of fluids. I don't think I really had to tell them that. Mike looked like those pictures of people dying of dehydration in Africa.

When the surgery was over, his regular surgeon told me that they had problems in surgery with his blood pressure. He told me that Mike's kidneys were shutting down, he was dehydrated, septic, and he had pneumonia. The surgeon had decided to keep the breathing tube in him and keep him on the ventilator when the surgery was over. He spoke tentatively, as if I would be disappointed or shocked. I was relieved and a little surprised that Mike was still alive.

The anesthesia team saved his life that day in surgery. They observed him, monitored him, and gave him fluids. If he had spent many more hours on the burn ward in the condition he was in, he would have died. Sometimes when people tell me they are afraid of surgery or anesthesia, I remember the day the anesthesia team saved my son's life, and reassure them that they are quite safe.

Over the next two days, even with the fluids and antibiotics he was finally receiving, Mike developed Adult Respiratory Distress Syndrome (ARDS). This life-threatening condition develops in seriously ill patients. The membranes of the person's lungs become swollen and stiff and can no longer function to exchange the oxygen and carbon dioxide necessary for life. A certain percentage of people never recover from this. The burn team recruited more ICU specialists to help adjust his respirator settings to maximize the oxygen exchange in the lungs. Up until this point, he had had one-on-one nursing care. They now started assigning him two, sometimes three nurses, around the clock to keep him alive. The nurses told us that he was the sickest patient in the hospital.

They gave him medicine to paralyze his muscles, so he wouldn't fight the respirator's actions in breathing for him. It was one more thing for me to worry about. Usually patients on respirators with a tube in their mouth can still communicate many things. They can write; they can express feelings with their eyes and hand motions. They can shake or nod their heads.

They can mouth words over the tube. Increased restlessness or facial grimaces will tell the nurse that the person is experiencing pain. All those methods of communicating pain are gone if a person's muscles are paralyzed. I worried about Mike being in extreme pain, and only he would be aware of the pain, totally unable to communicate it.

I kept reminding the nurses when it was time for more pain medication, and making sure they gave it. I had changed. The prior weekend had taught me that I couldn't trust the staff to see when Mike was in trouble and an intervention was needed. I do need to clarify that there were some clinicians caring for Mike that I trusted very much, but there were also some that needed careful monitoring. I needed to make them see. I had to make them see. I became more vocal and more demanding. I had learned that I needed to be the nurse first and not just his mother if he was going to live. I studied articles on burn care. I began to check everything, watching everything like a hawk. I became the dread nurse-mother breathing down their necks.

A WALK WITH GOD

I read about a man who'd been sentenced to die,
saying or thinking, the hour before his death,
that even if he had to live somewhere high up
on a rock...with all around precipices, an ocean,
an endless murk, endless solitude, and endless
storms—and had to stand there, on those two
feet of space, all his life, for a thousand years,
eternity—that it would be better to live like
that than to die so very soon! If only he could
live, live, and live! Never mind what that life
was like! As long as he could live!

Fyodor Dostoyevsky

Every day we would go into Mike's room hoping for
a change. Some days he would seem a little better,
and we would be hopeful that he had turned a corner,
only to have everything degenerate overnight or within
a few hours. The overall depressing trend each day was
higher respirator and oxygen settings and worsening

blood gases (levels of oxygen and carbon dioxide in the blood). I watched the intensive care specialist come into his room every day. He surveyed the scene of Mike wrapped head to toe in soupy, bloody gauze, hooked up to the respirator, attached to multiple monitors, multiple tubes, and bags of IV fluids. He would look at the respirator settings and then just stand there for the longest time, looking and shaking his head sadly before walking out of the room.

They experimented with a variety of respirator settings and a variety of respirators. One day I walked into his room and he was on a respirator that just vibrated his chest. It was loud and scary. I didn't like the fact that it didn't breathe in and out in a normal breathing pattern like a regular respirator. This machine did not even mimic life.

The ARDS continued to progress, complicated by pneumonia and a collapsed lung. When they placed a chest tube in his chest to re-expand his collapsed lung, he almost died. Usually this is a routine procedure with few complications. I am not sure what happened with Mike that day, but I know they had difficulty resuscitating him.

Once they had Mike stabilized, the surgeon met with us privately. He said very quietly, "I have cared for many burn patients. Your son's lungs are so damaged at this point, that I am afraid that if he lives, he will live only to be respirator dependent. I am recommending that you make him 'DNR.'" Those letters stand for "Do Not Resuscitate," meaning that if his heart stopped beating, they wouldn't use any heroic measures such as CPR or electric shock to get his heart pumping again. We agreed that it was the sensible, logical choice. We prepared family and friends for the possibility that he might not survive. Because I could discuss it rationally, I thought that I had accepted this possibility. We started tentatively discussing his funeral.

During the next few weeks, Mike's life dangled over the precipice. In addition to his kidneys, his liver started failing. Some days we prepared our hearts for his death, other days for the long, arduous journey that life as a burn survivor would mean. His brothers found it difficult to visit him and see him in this condition, so we kept them posted each night when we arrived home from the hospital. We did not know how to prepare them for his death.

On one of the days when he seemed to be teetering more than usual on the edge of life, I told my youngest son before he went off to school that Mike might not make it through the day. Then, I worried all day. Was it wisdom to lay that burden on his shoulders? Would anxiety over his brother interfere with his schoolwork? Was it better for him to start preparing his heart now, or did my words serve only to kill hope?

Mike still needed surgery, even in his critical condition. If there was any chance for his survival, it was necessary to continue removing the necrotic-burned skin and to cover his body with skin grafts. One day they were getting him ready for transport to surgery and clamped off his chest tube from the suction that was keeping the lung expanded. As soon as the tube was clamped, his right lung collapsed again. He became agitated, fighting and gasping for air, and then he turned blue. His heart rate on the monitor became erratic and bizarre. He was dying again! His heart wasn't getting the oxygen it needed to pump the blood to the rest of his body.

Over the next few moments, they pumped his lungs with oxygen, re-attached the chest tube to wall suction, and gradually he pinked up again. His heart remained in an erratic rhythm. During those moments watching him turn blue and struggle for breath, I was convinced that this was the moment of his death. I felt the same terror I experienced the first few times he stopped breathing as an infant. Until that moment, I believed that I had accepted the prospect of his death, but standing there and watching him minutes from slipping away from this earth again, everything in me screamed, *No—not this, not this, not now!*

Once stabilized, he went to surgery, and I went for a long walk in the cold, soggy spring woods. I tried to calm myself down, reminding myself that Mike was safe in God's hands—the only place any of us ever need to be, whether here on earth or in heaven. As I slogged through the mud, with the skunk cabbage and some brave ferns waking up from their winter sleep, I prayed. I stepped over dead branches strewn haphazardly from winter storms. Naked tree branches scraped the steel gray sky as the wind blew.

As I prayed, I heard God question me, "What do you want me to do with Mike's life?" It was a scary question, because I felt that God had really placed the choice of whether to let Mike go or have him live into my hands at that moment. Sometimes when I pray, God seems far away. My prayers seem to bounce off the ceiling or float untethered in the universe. There are other times, though, when God seems very close, and we have heart-to-heart conversations. This was one of those times. I believe that at that point, if I had prayed for him to die, he would have died in surgery that day.

As I walked, I waffled in my discussions with God. I did not know what to ask for. I believe in eternal life. I knew logically that death, after all he had suffered so far in this life, would be a kinder, more compassionate option. I remembered patients who had recounted to me their near-death experiences, and I remembered my own mini-one on the evening that he was born. Death is not the end.

His life had been so difficult to this point—what would life as a burn survivor entail? At the very best, he would have disfiguring scars all over his body. Would his lungs ever be the same? Would he recover just enough to be respirator dependent? Would he ever be able to run and play basketball and swim again? His right hand had been damaged during the hospitalization, and it just flopped around without any muscle tone. Would that gimpy right hand ever be able to hold anything again? What about his psychiatric difficulties? Would the catatonic depression return once the burn crisis had passed? It seemed to make the most sense for God to take him to heaven.

As I sloshed through the mud, I found I could not make that sensible, rational, compassionate choice. When I started imagining the rest of my life, our family's life, without Mike being part of the journey, my eyes flooded with tears. I remembered his laughter and his smile, how he always wanted our family together. I remembered his love and tenderness for his two brothers. I remembered how much I loved him. I kept remembering how much I loved him. Perhaps, even now there could still be a possibility of a future full of hope for him in this world. Perhaps there will be a future day, when Mike will wake up on a spring morning and hear the birds chirping, and he will think that all his sufferings were worth it.

I know that love often requires letting go. After walking and talking for an hour or so, I realized that I couldn't— even in these dire straits, even when letting go was the more loving, compassionate option—pray for God to take him. Death is final, permanent. Yes, in faith I believe that heaven is better, but I was not able to let go, to say good-bye. I could not do it. I still had hope, still believed that a good life was possible for him on this earth.

I work with dialysis patients, and often toward the end of a person's life, a person's body starts shutting down bit by bit, causing so much suffering. The question often in the minds of the staff caring for them is, *What kind of life is this?* I remember many times as a nurse working in acute dialysis, when with a particularly sick patient, I would look at one of my co-workers with my forehead wrinkled and my eyes wide with alarm, and quietly mouth the words, "What the hell are we doing, dialyzing this corpse?"

There is a joke in the dialysis community about an oncologist who had a patient who died of cancer. A week after his patient died, he discovered a new treatment that might have saved him, so he went to the cemetery to dig up his patient's body. When he opened the casket, he found that it was empty, except for a note inside stating, "Gone to dialysis."

Dialysis is a double-edged sword. It is a wonderful technology for preserving life. However, toward the end of a life, the same wonderful technology prolongs suffering mercilessly, interfering with the prospect of a peaceful death. When dialysis was a new therapy, people created these ethical dilemmas, thinking that withdrawal from dialysis was a form of euthanasia. Over the years, after much ethical wrangling, the consensus developed that there comes a point where dialysis becomes futile. It no longer supports life, but prolongs the dying process. Identifying that exact point, however, is difficult. The decision to withdraw from dialysis is left to the patient and family to decide. Though many patients and their families will discuss the option of stopping dialysis (and dying) and assent to its reasonableness, few actually withdraw. I suspect it is because of the two great unknowns, death and tomorrow. No one can say for certain what it is like to die, and no one knows what possible good tomorrow might bring.

Earlier that winter, one of my patients, an elderly woman, told me she wanted to stop dialysis. She no longer had any legs. She had lost them inch by inch to amputations performed for poor circulation and infections. She suffered unrelenting pain, living totally dependent in a nursing home. Her husband didn't want her to stop though, so she hung around a little longer. Every day he came to visit her at the nursing home, and they ate dinner together. Well, he ate; she had a tube feeding because she could not eat.

Before this time with Mike, I judged the husband as being selfish, wanting to have her near, even at the cost of her suffering and pain. Now I understood. I could not let Mike go either, even when his remaining on earth meant suffering for him and us. I understood the ambivalence with turning off the technology that prolongs the dying process. My mind grasped and understood the sensible, compassionate logic of letting him go, but my heart still clung to his life.

The heart is not a logical organ.

The reader might be wondering after reading about these discussions with God whether perhaps there might be a nice bed waiting for me in a psychiatric ward somewhere. "Hearing the voice of God" is an ancient problem. Human history is replete with stories of people in power using God's authority and words to control others for their own ends. There have been and continue to be so many wars and killings done in God's name. So much evil has been promulgated with this taking of God's name in vain in big and small ways. It is a major problem, this attributing to God our own self-centered thoughts and desires.

There is also the issue of psychiatric illness. A little change in the mixture of neurotransmitters in the brain, the dopamine, serotonin, norepinephrine and others that we don't even know about, and a person will start hearing voices from people not talking to them. When psychiatric patients start reporting that God is talking to them, it is usually time for a medication adjustment. Because of all these and many more problems with "hearing God's voice," it is tempting to dismiss the entire phenomenon and conclude that God doesn't ordinarily speak to people, or that He used to speak, but stopped thousands of years ago.

But what if God desires to speak with us more than we want to hear? The scriptures equate God with being the Word and with being Love. Because God identifies Himself with two key essentials of communication, it is possible that even with all these problems in communicating with humans that He still desires to speak, still desires relationships that depend on communication. In the story of the fall, when Adam and Eve were hiding from God, God was still looking for them and calling to them to walk in the cool of the evening with Him, even knowing that they had disobeyed his command.

There is an African oral tradition, the Bambara tradition of the Komo. In this tradition, the Word is a fundamental force emanating from the Supreme Being. In their myth of creation, the Supreme Being created man because He wanted someone to talk to. A great mystery of faith is that the Master and Creator of the universe wants to communicate with us personally. Jesus called his disciples his friends. I believe God speaks to us all the time, but these days most of us are too noisy and too busy to hear. We still hide from Him when He calls our name.

Even when we are actively trying to listen to God, believing in faith that He speaks, there are difficulties. Even when we take the time to pray and listen, we won't ever hear and understand His communications perfectly while we still live in this flesh in this world. This is not a good reason to dismiss the entire phenomenon though.

Every relationship has times of not understanding and poor communication. We have difficulties speaking face to face, human to human. Daily we misunderstand and misconstrue communications with each other. It is even more difficult between divine and human. Who can understand the mind of God? The walk of faith is always a bit uncertain. I love the stories of Jesus's interactions with his disciples. How frequently they misunderstood him even when they could see and touch him! I listen and talk to God, knowing that many times I won't hear correctly or understand. Sometimes I don't hear a thing; sometimes His Words get all tangled in the brambles of my fears and desires. Other times we walk in the cool of the garden together.

BIRTHDAY PARTIES

I'm lost in the middle of my birthday. I want my
friends, their touch, with the earth's last love. I
will take life's final offering, I will take the last
human blessing. [29]

Rabindranath Tagore

On Mike's birthday, I found myself sitting at
his bedside, remembering his birth and past
birthdays, the toys, excitement, games we played, and
his childhood friends. When the tub team came in to
scrub him and change his dressings, they sang "Happy
Birthday" to him. I cried. I had only wanted good for
his life, had always worked to make his birthdays happy
days for him, and this was one sorry, sad, gruesome
birthday party.

He was still so sick, his life so tenuous. I was
superstitious that he would die on his birthday. Even
though I had told God that day when we walked
together in the spring woods that I wouldn't be able

to release him easily to die, I still wasn't certain at this point that he would actually survive. You never really know for sure, 100 percent without a doubt, if you have heard God correctly.

A few days later, two of Mike's childhood friends came home from college for spring break. They wanted to visit Mike. I tried to discourage their visit because he looked so bad with so many tubes, and he couldn't talk to them anyway. He was covered with bloody gauze bandages. He looked horrible. But they said they *had* to see him. These young men had known and played with Mike since they were seven years old or so. They had moved into our neighborhood when Mike had been praying for friends.

Their mother is a nurse, and I suspect she told them before they came to visit that even if he couldn't respond, he could hear. They walked into his hospital room and each took one of his limp hands. With tears in their eyes, they started remembering for him the fun they had growing up—neighborhood sports games, capture the flag on summer evenings, tree forts, sled riding, swimming in ponds, and then some of the teenage adventures that I didn't want to know about. There were so many good memories.

Mike couldn't move any of his muscles or say anything back to his friends. He did open his one eye that wasn't taped shut and kept it open the entire time they were there. Who knows if Mike was aware of their presence? However, I knew they were there and was so blessed and comforted by their visit. As I sat there watching, my eyes filled with tears over the love these young men showed my son. Even with all his problems before the burn, they reminded me of all the goodness, mercy, and laughter that had been a part of Mike's life.

An earlier birthday party

Shortly after that, the burn team decided to start him on steroids as a last ditch effort to salvage his lungs and his life. This was a risky proposition for a burn patient, because it increases the risk for life-threatening infections, and the research studies don't suggest that steroids have much effect. However, within two days, Mike started to improve. They began turning down the respirator settings, and bit by bit, the oxygen levels in his blood began to increase. They stopped paralyzing him. Hope returned. It was refreshing to walk into Mike's room in the morning and see the celebratory looks on the faces of the nurses. In retrospect, we weren't the only ones who had been losing hope.

My husband and I were tired to the core—too many days spent in his hospital room. We not only knew the names of the nurses, respiratory therapists, physical therapists, and housekeeping staff, but had developed nicknames and code names for many of them such as: "Biker Chick," "Battleaxe," and "Mrs. Flanagan." I am sure the staff also had a few nicknames for us. I don't think I want to learn what they were.

During all this time, Mike continued to go to surgery at least once a week in the attempt to get more of his own skin on. They began to harvest skin a second time from previously harvested sites as soon as they had healed over enough. The nurses told us that the pain from the doubly harvested sites was worse than any pain he had experienced so far from the burns. They also needed to replace previously grafted skin that had sloughed off with all his infections. At this time, they also started preparing us for the eventuality of putting a tracheostomy in his neck because he had been on a respirator for so long. A tracheostomy again! I thought we dispensed with that proposition when he was a baby!

The nurse who cared for Mike that week was one that my husband and I had named "Biker Chick" because she was so tough. She was nonchalant about the idea of my son being trached. My husband developed a pantomime of this nurse smoking a cigarette and then spitting as she said with a snarl, "Trach him," and when Art did it, I would laugh hysterically. Mike never got the tracheostomy though. The skin grafts in his neck had sloughed off, and there wasn't a skin barrier in place to protect his neck from the secretions from a trach. He was off the respirator long before any skin grew on his neck.

The next few weeks were spent waiting and watching. There were some calm, hopeful days interspersed with intermittent crises. I spent entire days at his bedside reading and correcting students' papers as the respirator sighed a mechanical harsh rhythm. When Mike woke up, he would attempt to communicate by mouthing words around his endotrachial tube. It is difficult to lip read when there is a huge tube coming out of the center of a person's mouth. Sometimes when a patient is intubated, he or she can write out their wishes and thoughts on clipboards. Those early days Mike didn't have the strength to hold a pencil. Most of the time I had no idea what he was trying to say, but his eyes communicated the words, "Get me the hell out of here!" or something along those lines. Those days were hard because I really didn't know what he was aware of, or what he thought of all this pain, or what he would remember. The nurses tried to reassure me, telling me that he would remember nothing.

As time progressed, Mike would wake and struggle to work the TV controller. He refused to let me help him, wanting to be able to do something by himself. For a few days, the TV screen remained black and blank. Eventually he figured it out and would surf the channels. All through the early weeks of the burn, we played music for him, mostly Christian worship music, hoping to soothe his soul and spirit and help along the healing process as much as possible. I hoped the music would send subliminal messages to his soul and spirit that he was loved. That music was the first thing he figured out how to turn off.

I longed to speak with him and hear his voice. I had so many questions. No longer did I ruminate over possible funeral arrangements; now the questions concerned what he would remember and what he would be like when he really woke up and started talking. What was he thinking about all this? Would he be grateful for all the work, care, prayers, more than seventy blood transfusions, and money that people who knew him and people who did not poured into him these past months to keep him alive? Would he be grateful for this second gift of life? How much of his pain and troubles did he even understand? How would he react to the scarring? Was he experiencing all of this in a normal state, or was he still psychotic after all of this?

During the weeks up to the burn, the psychiatrist had been suggesting electric shock therapy (ECT). It is another one of those drastic interventions, like a tracheostomy, that one would like to avoid at all costs. However, at times, it is useful, and psychiatrists resort to it because it works. But surely, I reasoned, the burn itself, the multiple surgeries, the weeks of septic shock, the weeks his lungs didn't work, the insulin shock (which also happened), and the collapsed lungs would have had the same effect as shock therapy.

We waited and wondered. We waited for his lungs and skin grafts to start healing. We waited for the time when he no longer needed a respirator and the tube could come out of his mouth and he would be able to speak again. Though we were waiting for many things, it was to hear him speak again that we wanted most of all. Mike was never much of a talker. In fact, most of his life we were trying to get him to tell the stories of what it was like to live behind his eyes and in his head and heart. Sometimes when he was growing up and we would ask him a question, he would be silent or get irritated because he didn't know how to respond, but then a week later, randomly (usually when I was busy and concentrating on something else), he would answer the question.

The summer before the burn, while Mike was still in the Cadet program before heading to Chicago, he started writing a book, telling stories of what he had learned during his teen years. It was along the lines of, "Now that I am older and wiser, take my advice and don't do drugs and some of the other stupid things I did." Some of his writings were typical of the angst of a young teenager. He wanted to make sense of his life. He wanted independence and to be master of his own fate. He wanted a girlfriend to love him.

I tried to keep the book in one place, but because of his developmental disability, overlapping the bipolar disorder, and compounded by Attention Deficit Disorder, it was a stretch to call it a book. I discovered pages scattered under his bed, in laundry baskets, in kitchen drawers, and under the floor mats in my car. Parts of the book were on the computer, sometimes imbedded in some of the work I was doing. Sometimes there were just one or two sentences on a page. Sometimes he filled the whole page with writing; sometimes he wrote in complete sentences; sometimes he just scratched random thoughts and feelings. On some days his handwriting was legible; other days it wasn't. Sometimes his writing was coherent and insightful; other times it was incomprehensible. Perhaps only Mike and I could, with a straight face, call it a book. I thought of those pages as treasures, hints as to what was transpiring in his heart and mind. The multiple pages scattered and crumpled in drawers, cars, under beds, and underfoot intimated at the daily chaos in his mind.

The days of waiting in the burn unit now were quiet. He was awake, and his vital signs were stable. His right hand was splinted, and occupational therapists and physical therapists performed exercises to prevent skin contractures. His left eye had completely healed from the corneal infection. At this point, Mike no longer wanted to hold my hand as he did earlier when he was so sick and afraid. He just pushed it away.

He was so weak he could lift his legs only half an inch or so above the mattress. Intravenous lines, respirator tubing, and rectal and Foley catheter tubing all restrained him. Someone who hadn't been in bed for the past eight weeks or so might fight the tubes and try to get out of bed, but those days were long past for Mike, and a certain acceptance had settled in.

Even with this new hope and progress, there were still minor crises. After one such peaceful day, Art and I had a relaxed dinner at the home of some friends. We shared news about Mike's progress and improvements. When we returned to the hospital to check on him before we went to bed, we discovered a swarm of nurses around his bed. He had had another emergency chest tube insertion for a new tension pneumothorax (hole in his lungs) that was causing his oxygen levels to drop again and his trachea and heart to deviate to the left. He already had one chest tube from the first pneumothorax; now there were two on that side. I became scared, wondering just how fragile his lungs had become.

Finally, on a Wednesday morning, after several days of waiting and flunking the different readiness tests, they finally removed his endotracheal tube and took him off the respirator. As soon as the tube was removed, he started begging for pizza, hamburgers, and shrimp. However, his appetite was quickly suppressed by a little bit of Jell-O, and he didn't talk pizza again for a few months.

ICU PSYCHOSIS

A question that sometimes drives me hazy: am
I or are the others crazy?[30]

Albert Einstein

In nursing school, we learned about ICU psychosis.
This condition happens to patients who have been
in an ICU for any length of time. They become sleep
deprived and confuse days and nights. Usually there
are no windows to help differentiate the days from the
evenings. The activity levels in the unit remain constant
regardless of day or night. Lights are on all the time.
I spent the night in the hospital on the day of Mike's
extubation, because the nurses told us that he had
become anxious, his oxygen levels dropped, and he had
a harder time breathing when I was gone. The first day
off the respirator was quite tenuous.

Mike had not slept at all for over twenty-four hours,
so I was hopeful that he (and I) would get some sleep
that night. However, every time he started to drift

off to sleep, the nurse woke him up for something: a blood sugar test, a blood pressure reading, eye drops, treatments, and medications. By 3:00 a.m., I had become a raving lunatic, and I lost it with the nurse. I told her to use her nursing judgment. He didn't need hourly blood pressures if he was sleeping and the heart monitor and pulse ox were steady; he didn't need eye drops to lubricate his eyes if his eyes were closed; blood sugars could be drawn from one of his lines so he wouldn't be awakened for a finger stick. I asked her (not very nicely) then to do everything else she needed to accomplish that night while he was awake, so she wouldn't have to awaken him (and me) again. I then apologized for losing it with her and thought the rest of the night would be quiet.

I woke at 4 a.m. to the sounds of Mike moaning and yelling, because she did his 4 a.m. bowel irrigation. (Yes, you read correctly—a bowel irrigation, a giant enema!) He had this tube in his rectum, and they were irrigating it with one half liter of fluid three times daily. Sometimes it worked well to keep his dressings clean; sometimes it did not. This time it did not. Mike was yelling and moaning because of the abdominal cramping and because the stool was leaking all around the tube and onto his grafts and wounds and causing him pain. The next hour was spent with three nurses and me moving him back and forth cleaning his wounds and changing all his dressings and bed linens. At 5 a.m., after he had been cleansed and all his linens changed, I was hoping for at least one or two hours of sleep.

At 5:30 a.m., two respiratory therapists came in with needles to obtain a blood gas. (For those readers who don't know what a blood gas is, a needle is stuck in the radial artery by the wrist. The artery runs parallel to a branch of the radial nerve. So, frequently, it is the nerve that gets stuck with the needle. It can be very painful.) After watching two respiratory therapists dig that needle in and out of the wrist of his limp right hand for an interminable amount of time and coming up dry, with Mike wincing and yelping, I asked them to leave and not come back nor send anyone else in. Less than fifteen minutes later, the portable chest x-ray machine rumbled into the room. They torture prisoners of war with sleep deprivation. I became a screaming, raging lunatic.

I spoke with his surgeon that morning, describing Mike's night schedule. He stopped all the nighttime orders or rearranged them to daytime, and wrote an order for an official bedtime at 10:00 p.m. If I had not spent that night, how long would this sleep-depriving torture have continued? Why did this need to be a doctor's order? A 10 p.m. bedtime with no interruptions should have been a nursing decision. Good sleep is so necessary to the healing process.

Those months of sitting at Mike's bedside gave me many opportunities to observe hospital nursing care in this age of technology. I saw some excellent nursing care and some other care that made me sad for the profession. I have always loved being a nurse. It is my opinion that nursing is a profession very close to the heart of God. I have always felt closer to God at the bedside of a patient than I ever felt in a church service. As a nurse, I am grateful for the privilege of a sitting in front row pew in some crucial moments in other people's stories.

Nurses are the unsung heroes who save patients' lives. Because nurses are with the patients the most, they are most often the ones to recognize early subtle changes in the patient and then intervene to prevent a crisis or deterioration. Other times they can arrange the environment to keep the sick person (and family members) calm and comfortable, so the body and spirit can heal.

I had not worked in a hospital for many years and was dismayed to observe the rote performance of doctor's orders without the critical assessment of their effect on the patient. Too much focus was on the machines and numbers, and too little focus on Mike's actual physical condition. For example, before the crisis with his blood infection and failing lungs, the nurse caring for Mike was quite comfortable with his respiratory rate of fifty and difficulty breathing, because the oxygen monitor on his finger measured the oxygen levels in his blood at a good range. Sometimes the numbers lie, and you have to look at the patient.

Many of the nurses were compassionate, but a few took care of him as if they were servicing a car—like the twelve-point inspection at Jiffy Lube. Empty the oil, fill it up, oil the door hinges, check the tire pressures, and mark off the checklist. In one week, unobservant nursing care led to an ulcerated cornea in his eye and wrist drop. Another time he went into insulin shock because the insulin drip was set at ten times the rate it should have been. It could have killed him. I was the one who noticed.

I do understand rote nursing care. The work of nursing is physically and emotionally exhausting. There are more tasks than are humanly possible to accomplish each shift. Sometimes a nurse has to numb herself to a patient's suffering in order to get the job done. To see a patient's suffering, and feel so powerless before it, can be paralyzing. However, some nurses took great care of Mike. We loved it when they were assigned to him. He was comfortable and did well on their shift. They were able to see Mike as a person in spite of all the machines and tasks surrounding his care.

The nurse that took care of him that night was an experienced nurse and technically competent. I believe (hope) she knew on some level that a bowel irrigation at 4:00 a.m. on a sleep-deprived person with his sleep-deprived mother (who was also a nurse), in the same room was not a good idea. I suspect she was afraid not to do it because of doctors' orders. Why, in these days of medical advances and constant changes in health care roles, are nurses still unthinkingly following doctor's orders to a T?

Nowadays, nurses are required to check off a computer checklist as every doctor's order is completed. A friend of mine who is a new nurse told me that her evaluations focus solely on whether she is able to accomplish all the tasks on the checklists efficiently. That is too bad, because there is an unquantifiable art to nursing. So much of nursing has nothing to do with the tasks surrounding the care.

The checklist may be perfect, but it is not an accurate indicator of excellent nursing care. How can you measure compassion or wisdom? There are no checklists for a gentle touch or the right word in a moment of crises. How can you quantify comfort and the sense of safety that takes away fear? How do you reward timely observations and interventions before a patient crashes? How do you identify patient advocacy and crises averted? An averted crisis is almost always unnoticed.

THE ROAD BACK

"Healing," Papa would tell me, "is not a science,
but the intuitive art of wooing nature."[31]

W.H. Auden

Two days later, his two chest tubes were removed,
and a few days after that, his colon irrigation system
was discontinued. The removal of the big tubes marked
the beginning stages of rehabilitation. After so many
weeks of immobility, Mike's muscles had shriveled; he
could barely move his legs. In spite of all the work of the
nurses, physical therapists, and occupational therapists,
his shoulders had contractures from the burns. He had
limited arm movement. His right hand remained limp
and useless. He had lost over thirty pounds.

Those beginning stages of rehabilitation were
difficult, because he had learned over the previous few
weeks that if he stayed very still, nothing hurt. It was
difficult to convince him that "comfortable" was not the
goal at this point; moving again was. At this point in

his recovery, he still needed one more surgery to get more of his skin on, but it was necessary to wait for the donor sites to heal on his own body. They had harvested them twice already, and each time the donor sites hurt a little more and took longer to heal. He still needed transfusions, and infections and pneumonia were still possibilities. He wasn't entirely out of the woods yet, but the big trees were thinning, and patches of sunlight were dappling the forest floor.

For my husband and me, the weeks blended into one long, amorphous day. I imagined ruts in the interstate highway where we had driven the same path, switching the same lanes two to three times a day for the past few months. We suffered burn unit "burn out." So many patients had come and gone during Mike's long ordeal that we stopped meeting or learning the names of the newly admitted ones. We didn't care anymore; we were burned out and just wanted to get all of us out of there.

There were many long days in Mike's hospital room, watching his futile attempts to take a few bites and keep it down without vomiting. He was hungry, but nausea, gagging, vomiting, and diarrhea were a constant frustration. His muscles and wounds hurt; his joints were stiff and painful to move. He still needed oxygen and struggled with anxiety. Even with the staff complicit with the goal of minimal nighttime interruptions, there were many sleepless, restless nights. Mike was very cooperative with the cute, young nurses, thanking them so sweetly that one of them told me tears came to her eyes. In fact, he was much more communicative and accommodating to the nurses than to Art and me. He knew who had the power, or at least who had the morphine.

They started getting Mike up in a chair. He would eat little bites here and there. I cannot describe the visceral maternal pleasure it gave me to see him eat. It is a mom thing. I think after so many weeks of tube feedings and brushes with death, just to see him take a bite of food brought such joy.

He started asking, "What am I going to do with my life?" That is the perennial human question. We all have ideas and goals, but sometimes they are erased and rewritten by life's tsunamis. We told him that every twenty-two-year-old person asked that question, and that it gets answered one day at a time, by living into it. I had been asking that question about his life since he was a child and was asking about it myself in the face of the burn. What can he do with his life now—with a chromosome deletion, a developmental disability, bipolar disorder, and now 60-percent burn? How would he find his purpose and be happy?

> I can't figure out my future. It seems like everyone's got it figured out but me. I want to do something with my life but I can't seem to put it together yet. The thing is, no one knows about their future. I mean, what is my life about? I just can't seem to figure it out.
>
> Mike

Even though he was slowly improving, there were still setbacks. One Friday spring afternoon as I was standing outside his room while Mike was using the bedpan, chatting with his surgeon, the nurse called for help in his room. Apparently, as he turned to get off the bedpan he went into respiratory distress. I watched my son turn blue and gasp for breath—again. As they were breathing for him with an AMBU bag, we realized that as he rolled off the bedpan, a large IV line, which was in a large vein in his chest, had just slid out. There wasn't any skin on his chest to suture the line to. When he took a breath in, the air from the room got sucked through the hole in his chest into his blood stream, giving him an air embolism. A chest x-ray shortly after showed that that assault had caused some pulmonary edema (extra fluid in his lungs).

He struggled to breathe the remainder of the night. For the next two days, he could not speak without needing to catch his breath, and needed a special mask that provided pressurized, moisturized oxygen. If this mask was off for only twenty-thirty seconds, the oxygen level in his blood would plummet to dangerous levels. I was hoping they wouldn't have to re-intubate him and put him back on the respirator. I did not like this recurrent "difficulty breathing" theme in his life. I had prepared my heart for his death a few weeks earlier (well, maybe not really), but as he had gotten better, letting go now was unbearable.

FORGIVENESS

If we could read the secret history of our enemies
we should find in each person's life, sorrow and
suffering enough to disarm all hostilities.[32]

Henry Wadsworth Longfellow

The following day was Saturday. Mike's regular surgeon was out of town again that weekend, and the one covering for him was the same one that dismissed my concerns the weekend Mike started dying. Not only that, Mike had the same nurse caring for him, the one who could not see that he was in trouble, even when I pointed out the problems to her. I panicked. All the fear and helplessness of that earlier weekend came rushing back. In addition to Mike's respiratory distress, I was also concerned about a possible upper airway swelling or abscess because of his seven-week intubation. His throat was hurting more each day, it was becoming increasingly difficult for him to swallow, he was suctioning purulent mucus out of his throat with handheld suction tubing, and he was choking on everything.

When the surgeon rounded that Saturday morning, I asked him if an ear, nose, and throat doctor could examine his throat because of all the problems he was having with breathing, with choking, and with swallowing. This surgeon casually glanced at his mouth from three feet away, without a light, and said. "Everything looks fine."

I went ballistic. "There is no way you can tell that everything is fine by glancing at his mouth from across the room! Do not blow me off as you did that weekend he became septic and went into ARDS!"

"It's people like you that make healthcare so expensive," he replied defensively.

"What do you mean by that?" I asked.

"Requesting unnecessary tests and consults," he answered.

"I think you have that wrong. If you had paid any attention at all that weekend that Mike crashed with sepsis and pneumonia, you could have saved thousands of ICU dollars for all the weeks that Mike needed three nurses around the clock to keep him alive!" I exclaimed.

"I don't want to take care of your son anymore," he said and walked out.

"That is *fine* with me," I retorted as the door closed behind him.

All during the weeks of suffering through the ARDS and the other sepsis complications, I had been obsessing, battling my heart and thoughts to forgive him for ignoring my concerns and not noticing that

Mike was septic, dehydrated, and had pneumonia. I also battled to forgive *myself* for not making more of a fuss until Mike received the care he needed. This argument with the doctor showed me how unsuccessful that endeavor was.

There was a slight problem with him not taking care of Mike anymore though. This surgeon was part of the burn group in the hospital and parting ways really was not an option for either of us, unless I was going to ship Mike to a different hospital. This surgeon was on call every third weekend. After the argument, the surgeon did order a CAT scan of his neck; it showed no abscess, so I was placated (a little).

In the weeks after Mike had developed ARDS, one of the nurses told me a story about this surgeon. This surgeon has a child with Down syndrome. Once, when he brought his child to the ER, the emergency room physician told him, "just be a dad, not a doctor." I am sure it was painful for him to have his concerns dismissed when they needed extra attention *because* he was both a father and a doctor. I understood then that he had treated me as someone had treated him, passing his pain on to me. So often in life, if we don't forgive and heal our own wounds, we are destined to just pass them on.

A few days later, we both found ourselves waiting to ride the same elevator. When I saw him standing next to me, I asked him if we could talk, and he agreed. We sat down next to each other on a grey vinyl bench next to the elevator.

"I am sorry I lost it with you on Saturday," I began. "I was scared because of his difficulties breathing, and we have been through so much. I guess I am tired and burned out."

"I know you think it was my fault that he crashed that weekend, but after he had all those complications, we reviewed his case to see if anything had been missed, or where we could have intervened earlier, and we couldn't find anything."

I nodded politely, thinking to myself, *No one asked me...I could have told you any number of places an intervention might have prevented Mike's crash.* I bit my tongue.

He went on. "Even with the most excellent care, bad outcomes can still occur. Sometimes, even when someone is very conscientious, mistakes still happen."

I nodded, remembering times in caring for patients where I missed something or made a mistake. Most of the time, the omission didn't cause a problem for the patient, but occasionally it did.

He went on, "I am a doctor because I care about people. I really love what I do, but many times, because I am human, I make mistakes. Not every error leads to a bad outcome; not everything done correctly leads to a perfect outcome. There is still so much in medicine that is outside of anyone's control."

I nodded and agreed, and we parted amicably, two health professionals understanding how difficult it is to take care of a sick patient, how easy it is, even when doing our best, to miss or overlook something. We were two parents with disabled children, hearts broken with love for them— two humans struggling and doing our best to get by in this world.

In retrospect, the issue was not medical errors or decision-making. The root of my anger was that no one had listened to me that weekend. Preconceived judgments had prevented the staff from hearing my concerns and then seeing the problem. I didn't say that to this doctor, although it may have benefited him.

Where does forgiveness begin or end? Who needs forgiveness? Maybe if the psychiatrist had prescribed the right medication earlier, Mike wouldn't have burned himself. The health insurance company was to blame for not allowing Mike to remain hospitalized until he was really better when he was starting little fires at home. (Actually, the insurance company paid hundreds of thousands of dollars for the few thousand dollars they saved by booting him out of the hospital after two days.)

However, I cannot get very far looking at other people's mistakes until I am face-to-face with some of my own very serious ones. How do I forgive myself for not seeing he was suicidal before the burn? It goes even further back—maybe the problem was sending him to Chicago before he was ready. Hadn't we learned from his prior experiment in leaving home? It really goes further and further back. So many mistakes I made, so many things I didn't know, didn't see, didn't understand. So many ways I could have loved Mike better and wiser.

If I forgive all the doctors, nurses, insurance companies, and myself, there is still more to forgive.

There is always more to forgive. I needed to forgive Mike for burning himself. Then there is God. My dear Friend, the Creator of the Universe, also needed my forgiveness for not answering my prayers, for not intervening to prevent the burn, and for creating Mike with a tiny chromosome deletion that would cause so much suffering for him.

There is a story in the gospel where Peter, thinking he had a grasp on the magnitude of the gospel's call to forgive, asked Jesus, "Lord, if my brother sins against me, how often must I forgive him? As many as seven times?" Jesus answered, "Not seven but seventy-seven times." (Mt 18:21-22).

After Jesus's resurrection, when he appeared to his disciples as they were huddled and fearful behind locked doors, he breathed peace on them and told them that those sins they forgave were forgiven. At that moment, they all experienced His forgiveness for being faithless friends and bad disciples. They had betrayed him, denied him, and run away fearful; they had forgotten the years they had walked with him. Perhaps Jesus's breathing of forgiveness was also a demonstration of how we are to forgive, with our every breath.

Forgiveness is as essential to life as breathing, moment by moment, breath by breath. It takes many years of struggle and practice to become a Grand Master in forgiveness. It is against our nature. Luckily, for most of us, the problems of our daily lives, especially living with other humans, provides ample fodder for such practice.

Many times in my life, I have gone through crises of faith, where I question most doctrines—not sure what is God's Truth and what is manmade truth. On those days, the one solid thing that I could always say for certain that I know, that I know, that I know, is the centrality of forgiveness to the gospel, to living with each other in this world, and living with God. Jesus was all about forgiveness, even on the cross; he forgave those who crucified Him. The scariest quote in the Bible to me is the one where Jesus ends His discourse on prayer by stating, "But if you do not forgive others, your Father will not forgive your failings either." (Matthew 6:15, JB).

Well, to be honest, that quote used to scare me, but not anymore. I believe that the same God who counts the hairs on our heads, the same God who forgave his crucifiers because they didn't know what they were doing, has an infinite capacity for forgiveness. Though he wants us to learn to forgive, for in forgiving we are most like Him, He will somehow manage to find an excuse to forgive us for our lapses in forgiveness.

WHEELCHAIR MUMMY

Oh, my friend, it's not what they take away
from you that counts. It's what you do with
what you have left.[33]

Hubert Humphrey

There was one final surgery for Mike, the eleventh.
This was the only surgery that Mike was aware
of; previously, he had been too sedated to be aware of
anything. He was scared. I tried to tell him that this
was nothing; he had had ten surgeries before this one.
He remembered nothing of the previous nine weeks.
He did not remember the pain, the surgeries, the daily
skin debridement, the chest tubes, and the respiratory
distress. He didn't even remember the nights the nurses
kept him awake. He remembered nothing. So, those
long weeks, he didn't need me at his bedside crying,
praying, talking to him, holding his hand, worrying
over his breathing and numbers. I guess I needed to be

there for myself. I couldn't have focused on anything else in my life anyway.

As he got stronger and I knew he would live, I was ready to return to ordinary life. I looked forward to returning to work and a regular schedule. As Mike woke up and discovered his new disabilities, he became anxious and needed me around. I complained in my heart about the long road ahead, but I also knew we were the lucky ones. Two burn patients had died since we arrived. The burn ward was located in a children's hospital. The cancer ward was full, and children died all the time there. Their families went home to face a bedroom full of toys and memories in every corner, and a cold and empty bed.

Eventually the time came when Mike had progressed to the point where he had to share his nurse with another patient. He continued to have pain in his graft sites, sometimes spiking slight fevers, but he was otherwise stable, drinking chicken broth and eating bites of mashed potatoes. He complained about lying in bed too long and wanted to come home. At this point, he was almost completely covered with his own skin, though it was red and bumpy. There were still patches of open sore areas needing healing. Scar tissue had caused contractures of his neck and shoulder. His muscles and wounds hurt, and all his joints were stiff and painful to move.

He needed help standing; two staff members had to hold him up. His legs were floppy and dangled like rag doll legs. His left hand worked, but it trembled so much it was pretty useless, and his right hand was limp, disconnected from his brain's instructions. It broke my heart to see him so feeble. Even though he was getting better day by day, I still cried, grieving the many losses: nice skin, a handsome face, good lungs, flexibility and strength, and the use of his hands. I grieved all the losses, not knowing which ones were permanent.

After so many weeks in the hospital, May and spring-time had come to Ohio, so I started taking him outside in his wheelchair. This helped his frustration and boredom. It helped mine also. I relished the escape from the burn ward. Mike made quite a sight along the streets of down-town Akron, wrapped up like a mummy in his wheel-chair with his scars, tubes, dressings, and few residual IV pumps attached to his wheelchair. Sometimes I would push his wheelchair around the empty ballpark, other times along the canal, and other times along Main Street with its businesses and eateries.

One day, as we were outside, a very kind and beautiful girl he knew from high school came to visit Mike and sit in the sunshine. She bought him a bag stuffed with hamburgers, fries, and hot fried jalapenos from a favorite drive-in fast-food restaurant. He ate the entire contents of the bag without one gag, retch, heave, or barf. All the while he smiled at her.

Though his body was in shambles, his spirits were good. There was not even a hint of psychosis. At times, he would grimace and complain about his frustrations with his stomach, the pain, and the hospital routines. That was a normal reaction to his situation. He also started telling us he didn't realize how much he was loved.

He said he knew that God was with him. Something at the core had changed. He was outgoing, open, and filled with gratitude. Perhaps it was the prayers of all the people praying for him. I imagined that with the more than seventy transfusions that he received during the burn crisis, that with each transfusion, a portion of each blood donor's generous spirit was transfused along with the red blood cells. I wondered if his mood was so good because they monitored his serum calcium levels daily, and this hospitalization was the first time in his life the levels were normal for an extended period of time.

The last weeks in the hospital, as he was slowly recovering, Mike's friends from high school, who were now home from college, started spending their evenings hanging out at his bedside, encouraging him instead of hanging out with girls and drinking beer. They made him music CDs and brought him movies to help pass the time. He had one friend with a giant, purple mohawk that the nurses were afraid to let into the hospital ward. They almost called security. I told them not to worry. He was working on his PhD in engineering and had a heart of solid gold. He brought in a rebuilt computer laptop that had belonged to his own father before he died. He was thinking Mike could use it to listen to music and watch movies. I will always remain grateful for the kindness of his friends as he started to recover. He needed them around more at that point than he needed me.

SISYPHUS

Any idiot can face a crisis; it is this day-to-day
living that wears you out.[34]

Anton Chekhov

I was really tired and I was just ready to go
home. I had been in the hospital a very long
time. I remember when our dog Kodo saw me,
she was so happy to see me. I was happy to be
home and happy to be alive.

Mike

They discharged Mike home after seventy-nine
days of hospitalization in the burn unit. Initially,
the burn team planned to send him to a rehab center
that was over an hour from our house. After some
negotiation, they offered us another option of outpatient
rehabilitation at the same hospital. Mike would be the
first patient in their new day rehab program. In the

outpatient rehab center they set up a home-like room where Mike would be able to eat and nap between exercise times during the days of rehab.

I drove him home on a warm, sunny day in June. Three staff members helped me get Mike into a wheelchair and then from the wheelchair to the car. It wasn't until we got home and I was alone getting Mike out of the car that I thought that maybe the three staff members should have come home with me. It took close to forty-five minutes, with Mike using a walker, to move from the car to the back porch where he could rest.

I was sitting on the back porch with Mike, planning the logistics of the next phase of the project, getting him into the house, when one of the neighborhood young men stopped by unexpectedly. He had known that Mike was coming home that day and saw our car in the driveway. He asked Mike if he wanted to come over to his house. So, before I could implement stage two of the plan, we got him and his walker into his friends' car at a much more rapid pace. Mike was motivated! He spent an hour or so visiting with his friend.

He had lost more than thirty pounds while in the hospital. Nausea, vomiting, and diarrhea were still problematic. One of the first things I did after he got home was go to a health food store. I scoured the aisles for high-calorie, high-protein, body-building supplements. These were not cheap. I drove home that evening with a car filled with over two-hundred-dollars worth of supplements. What in the world was I thinking?

Most of them tasted so bad, he couldn't consume them without gagging. A few years later, I disposed of most of them when cleaning out my kitchen cabinets. They had all gathered dust, crowding my shelves long past their expiration dates. It turns out that Mike really didn't need them anyway. Once he started to eat, he never stopped. He gained back his thirty pounds, and then some more—and now, with his big belly, we're trying to get him to cut back on his food intake.

Before discharge, he was fitted with Jobst burn garments. These are full-body elastic compression stockings. After a severe burn, the collagen in the skin forms at ten times the normal rate, causing raised red hypertrophic scarring and burn contractures. The goal of the compression garments is to prevent some of this. Any woman who has worn support hose can imagine the heat and discomfort of wearing a full body elastic stocking in the summer heat. They are much stiffer and less elastic than regular stockings and come in a variety of colors. Mike chose a variety of colors, but regardless of the color, they were ugly, enhancing his grotesque appearance. It was a bit scary to look at him. A few times he was stopped by the police because of his face mask.

Mike in his jobst garments and face mask

A few weeks after he had been home, he walked across the street to visit the new neighbors who had moved in while he was still in the burn unit. They had moved into the house where his best friend from childhood had lived. He had spent so many childhood hours playing and growing up in that house. We had sent the new neighbors cookies and introduced ourselves by note while Mike was in the hospital, but had not met them personally yet. They didn't know Mike. I think they became frightened when they saw the facemask and burn garments. They told him to go home and never come back again.

He wore those face and body stockings for over a year. He still has red, hypertrophic scarring and contractures. I wonder how bad the scars would have been had he not worn the elastic garments? Even with the hostile welcome of our new neighbors, he was never self-conscious about going into public with his scars and burn garments. It wasn't an issue. So many wasted worries about how he would react to the scars and deformities. He wasn't even interested in plastic surgery and laser surgery to help reduce the scarring. Sometimes I suspect the burn scars reflect his inner image of himself. There is now congruence where previously there was a discrepancy between his inner feelings and his outer appearance. He had always felt different from other people and now he looks different.

He continued to have problems with nausea, vomiting, and diarrhea, but the main problem during the early recovery period was itching! They say there is an itching that burn survivors experience that is deep and indescribable to those who haven't been burned. The grafted skin just doesn't quite fit right. It is bumpy, scarred, inflamed, leathery, and too tight. The burned nerve endings growing back could also be the source. Regardless of the cause, Mike scratched and scratched. If I spent two hundred dollars on dietary supplements, I spent a thousand dollars on various creams to control his itching. He would itch and itch and scratch to the point that he was creating new wounds and removing some hefty pieces of grafted skin. There is no way to exaggerate the number of interventions we tried to alleviate the itching and scratching. We used every cream, ointment, and spray on the drugstore shelf and over-the-counter and prescription antihistamines. We covered his hands with gloves and duct-taped his Jobst garments together. A friend came over and administered acupuncture. Nothing worked in the short term, but after a few years the itching subsided.

I forgot the sorrows and fears of the spring in the day-to-day labor of summer caregiving. It was a new stage. He needed so much physical care. He needed help with eating, walking, toileting, and bathing. It was akin to taking a newborn home, albeit a very large one. I was responsible for not only for his physical care, but also providing the ancillary services you would find in a rehab center. I was the dietary department, laundry department, and housekeeping services. It was exhausting.

Initially, bath time, with the requisite ointment, wound care, compression dressings, leg braces, and hand splints took three to four hours. After a few weeks, my husband and I developed a system and honed it down to two hours. All of it was tedious—the bathing, the skin and wound care, the burn garments, the hand splints, the leg braces, the laundry, the cleaning, the cooking, the driving back and forth from rehab, the doctors' appointments, and other chores.

I felt like Sisyphus in the old Greek myth. I don't remember what sins Sisyphus committed, but whatever he did, he was condemned in Hades to an eternity of futile labor. He was required to roll a huge boulder up a mountain, and when he almost made it to the top, the boulder would roll back down, and he'd have to start all over again. After a few months, I thought that Sisyphus had nothing on me as I tackled mountains of laundry, bloody sheets and clothes, dirty bathrooms,

Mike's messy bedroom, and the kitchen—over and over and over and over and over again, only to watch my work be decimated in minutes.

I learned to nap that summer, partially from exhaustion, but I suspect there was an element of depression at the loss of my life, time, and identity in the caregiving. The mantra that I developed during those first weeks of rehab was, "This is temporary; this is temporary. This too shall pass, like all of life's problems and joys."

Each step of independence for Mike was a hard-fought skirmish. Mike *enjoyed* the service and attention. Where the average person would be highly motivated to regain independence and function, Mike resisted. Once we thought he was able to do something, like put on his shirt or pull on his socks, we told him that he had to do it himself before he could go anywhere. Then agonized screaming, moaning, and groaning gushed from his room, sometimes lasting forty-five minutes or so. Anyone listening would believe he was in his final death throes (even we would start to wonder).

Then suddenly the racket would stop. My husband or I would then peek into his room just to be *sure* that he was still alive. We would find him sitting comfortably; successful in the task he had been assigned. The stakes really got high when we started to require chores again. Luckily, the neighbors lived a distance from our house, or I'm sure that we would have been reported for child abuse just from the racket.

After just a few weeks home, his friends started calling, and he'd go out with them. Did I tell you that

I love his friends? I was, and continue to be, blessed by their compassion and kindness to Mike. Even with the burn, the itching, the vomiting, and diarrhea, he enjoyed his life that summer. He went to parties, to ballgames, and out to eat. He played putt-putt golf. He saw many movies—as long as they didn't have fire in them. (We had to leave Fantastic Four in the middle because one of the gifts of one of the superheroes was being able to turn into fire. That was a little too close to a very bad memory for him.) A good friend of his from the PACE program in Chicago came and visited him for a week. The best part of having him so very much alive though was his laughter. He laughed again like when he was a baby. He would kid around, joke, and tease his brothers. He loved to yank his dad's and my chains. I loved, just loved to see him laughing.

He was also a bit hypomanic that summer. This is sometimes part of bipolar, where the person isn't psychotic manic, but has a hard time sitting still and concentrating on just one thing. We were starting to figure out a little of this bipolar pattern of mania in spring and summer and depression in the winter. Rehab caregiving for someone who is hypomanic tests the soul. He would want to eat, take a bath, go somewhere, exercise, call every one of his friends and relatives, want his neck rubbed, and then want to be left alone—all within a two-minute time frame. Initially we were delighted with his talkativeness and engagement with life after the winter of a catatonic depression, but after a few weeks of non-stop going from one thing to another, one idea and one thought to another, my husband and I looked at each other, squinted our eyes, and recognized, "Ah, it is summer mania season."

Overall, mania is more enjoyable than depression, although the constant commotion can be exhausting. There is also a problem with a person receiving so much focused attention. Mike started to believe that he needed it all the time. He would become angry, irritated, and abusive at times when things didn't go his way.

The spiritual and emotional landscape for me during this time was mixed, sort of like woods where fresh growth and flowers flourish among the old rotting logs. I was so very grateful for his life, and yet at the same time he was driving me crazy. I longed for freedom and time to myself.

During this time I continued to dwell in that silent abyss of unknowing that I had entered the first day of his burn. The silence that had started in so much pain and sorrow while sitting by Mike's bedside, persisted. It wasn't filled with pain and sorrow anymore, it was just full of...silence. This land of silence was a land of mystery. I don't know if this silence is an expected part of the healing process of a major trauma. Silence became my home.

Prior to the silence, I had loved the dancing and the worship of the charismatic church that we belonged to, but now it was too noisy. I craved silence. Silence in church, silence at home, silence in the car. Just silence. God was in the silence. Previously in my life, I had loved to drive listening to music, the news, or books on tape. I had always enjoyed having music playing in the background as I worked at home, but after the burn, for many months I dwelt in a deep silence in my heart. Noise was an irritation. I did talk with people and laugh, and engaged in life, but there was a parallel silence that I dwelt in that I couldn't describe or understand.

I remember distinctly when the silence ended and music returned. One evening when Mike was bored, I took him to a Borders bookstore. As Mike wandered around, I put on the headphones in the music department and started listening to various artists. I stood there listening to melodies and songs as if I had never heard music before. The melodies poured delight in waves into the deep crevices of my being. As I listened, tears streamed down my face. I wanted to stay there forever, listening to music. That night was a watershed. Music was back, and my capacity for enjoyment of it was richer and deeper than I could have imagined. I again fill my days listening to music, and the news, and books on tape, but sometimes I miss the peace and presence that I knew in that deep silence.

WAITING, WAITING, WAITING

All good things arrive unto them that wait—
and don't die in the meantime.[35]

Mark Twain

Most burn centers have burn support groups, where burn survivors commiserate, show their scars, and share their stories. We took Mike a few times the first few months he was home. It was the expected thing to do. We were told that Mike wasn't the only burn survivor; we were all burn survivors. Since he was hypomanic at this point, he couldn't sit still long enough to listen to the speaker and discussions, so he'd wander around the halls. I would be sitting at the meeting, trying to listen, pretending to be attentive, but inside I would be screaming, *Get me out of here!*

I know that we had survived a very serious burn, but I did not *want* to be a burn survivor, nor did I want to hang around other burn survivors. Because we were parents of a disabled child with mental illness, we already had more than our share of support groups to engage in. We had already spent hours in support meetings for parents of special needs children and special education support groups. We belonged to the Association for Retarded Citizens (ARC), and we belonged to the National Alliance for the Mentally Ill (NAMI). Our plate was full already. I would be listening to the stories of the other burn survivors, thinking cynically, *"It's only skin. You have your minds, your mental facilities. What is there to support about?"* It seemed so minor in the grand scheme of things.

Being a burn survivor pales in comparison to the day-to-day sorrows of living with someone with mental illness. Sometimes the symptoms of the distorted thinking and moods are so painful that the daily living in the relationship requires more resources than humans can muster up. Most of the time, mental illness does not end or heal up and scar like burnt skin. It is an ongoing battle fought every day for life. There was a time when we were nearing the end of Mike's burn hospitalization, and my husband and I were remarking how kind people have been to us—bringing food every night for eleven weeks, sending flowers and cards, taking us out to eat, and praying for us and for Mike. But then we looked at each other and said, yes, the burn was horrible, but it was also unbearable when Mike was lying catatonic on the couch waving his hand in front of his face for hours. There were days we could not engage him in life at all, let alone get him to go for a walk or to a movie. There were nights spent in suicide watches because I didn't want to wake up in the morning and find him dead. All these aberrations of mood and thought are such a hidden pain that only those who have gone through them or walked through them with a loved one have a hint as to the true ache and pain present. No one thinks to bring food and flowers to families with a loved one suffering from a mental illness.

After about five months of caregiving, Mike was getting stronger, and I wanted desperately to have my old life back. I was tired of the tedium and frustrated with caregiving. Mike was stronger and able to do many more things on his own. He was also beginning to become tired and frustrated with his disabilities. When asked to pick up clothes on the floor, he would swear at me. He would whine and fight any effort to get him to exercise or work on his rehab.

Those were days of waiting, waiting, waiting. We waited to wait. I waited in doctor's offices (his surgeon, psychiatrist, cardiologist, primary-care doctor, rehab doctor, psychologist, hand specialist, dentist, pulmonologist, gastroenterologist, and endocrinologist). I waited for nursing agencies to return phone calls, waited for approvals to come through, waited for Mike to start working at Goodwill, waited for evaluations, waited for the physical therapists to schedule their appointments, and waited for public transportation approval for Mike to get to work. I waited for Mike to stop yelling, waited for his wounds to heal, and waited for movement to come back to his right hand.

In November, Mike finally started working at Goodwill, a sheltered workshop, though not every day as I had hoped, but only for three hours, two days per week. This was not sufficient time to have him occupied enough for me to return to work. After a month, we had a meeting to discuss increasing his work hours. I was hoping that they would increase his hours, so I could develop a routine for myself and return to work. Taking care of patients or teaching is much more satisfying and rewarding than wiping poop off bathroom walls, cleaning toilet seats, and washing bloody sheets. At the meeting, they agreed to increase his days to three hours, three days per week for the next three months! When I objected to the plan, because Mike needed structure to his days—especially going into the dark cold days of winter—and I desperately wanted to return to work, they asked Mike if he wanted to work more. He said, "No," and that was it.

It was the self-determination philosophy rearing its ugly head again. At the meeting, I asked Mike what he planned to do the other two days as he was unable to structure his days and was quite bored at home. He just made faces at me. He had no answer, and the Goodwill social worker said that would be the problem for the MRDD social worker. Maybe she could find volunteer work for him. My husband, who was also at the meeting, was positive about the situation, stating that volunteer work would provide a nice variety for Mike's week.

Now I had been trying to find volunteer work for Mike for two months without success. I wondered, *If on the outside chance they could find some volunteer work for him, then what? Would a company or volunteer agency take him for two full days? Would he be an asset to the company, or as I suspected, an extra burden to them? Then, we would need to get a job coach to help him learn the job, which takes weeks, and then there was the transportation issue again that had yet to be resolved. It was difficult to obtain transportation to the Goodwill job now. How would I find transportation to a volunteer job?* I despaired.

Up to this point, the MRDD social worker hadn't been able to make anything happen. I hadn't been able to make anything happen. Every plan that seemed to be a possibility became a house of cards blown away—maybe never even quite a house, just one or two cards supporting each other before falling apart. I despaired.

I was depressed at the prospect of a winter with Mike yelling, refusing to clean up after himself, refusing attempts to get him to do his exercises, and making a pigsty in every room he set foot in. There were many hours spent each week transporting him, bathing him, dressing him, trying to feed him healthy food and not the junk that he preferred. I was tired of listening to him as he would yell for me, and then tell me not to look at him or touch him or to just "shut up."

Nobody at the meeting saw the day-to-day ordeal that I was struggling with, nor was there any offer of understanding or support, just an acknowledgement that they knew it was not what I wanted. I was polite as we left the meeting but really despairing. I truly love Mike with my whole heart, and would give my life for him. It's just that I had reached the end of the frayed thread by which I had been hanging.

Over his lifetime, there had been many group meetings with Mike present. During those meetings, I would never describe the actual daily difficulties. The goal was always to build his self-esteem and to enhance him in the eyes of those who would be providing services to him. I am not sure this is universal, but Art and I always tried to make Mike appear as lovable and endearing as possible so the teachers, coaches, caseworkers, and social workers would be happy to work with him. We expended a lot of energy trying to make him look and appear better, more competent and sociable than he actually was. As parents over the years, we learned to be a buffer between Mike's orneriness, messiness, lacks, and disabilities, and the world because we didn't want the world or even our extended family judging him. I don't know if this tendency to overcompensate, to try to make your child look better than he really is, is common among other parents of children with disabilities, but it was something my husband and I did habitually.

I remember one time when Mike was in high school and my brothers were going to take him on a camping trip with them—without us. As I was packing Mike for his trip, it dawned on me that I would not be around to make Mike look good, to help him tie his shoes and get his backpack ready in the morning. I was afraid that when my brothers found out what he was really like they would not love and accept him as they had in the past.

I called my brother Tim and described to him my fears. In his kindness, he reassured me that they would love him and care for him, however he was, and make sure he had the help he needed. When Tim was reading an early version of this book and got to this paragraph, he penciled on the side that having Mike camping with them was a great gift to them because his presence with them on this trip brought out all their love. This was one camping trip where they camped not just focusing on themselves.

As we left the Goodwill meeting and got into the car, Mike had a little temper tantrum because I wouldn't stop at Rally's for a hamburger and fries. Then he asked what was for dinner, and I snapped, "What does it matter? You won't eat it anyway." My husband shot me a critical look. I was in the lowest place that I had been in since the burn. I was so, so tired and worn out, and so very disappointed that Mike still didn't have a regular work schedule so I could have a normal life again. I was empty and desolate. There was nothing positive to see about the situation. Mike was very much alive, but I was dying.

My husband and Mike dropped me off at home, and they went on to a doctor's appointment. When I realized that I was all alone in the house and could cry without anyone hearing me, I was shocked by the plaintive wail that arose from the depths of my soul as

I set about cleaning the bathrooms and the rest of the house. I didn't stop crying for two days.

Sometimes I want to be so strong and think that I am patient, kind, and loving, but I had reached the limit. Most of the time, I believe that God knows all the little details, not just the big picture, and that even the hairs on our head are counted, but I didn't believe anything on this day.

I felt forgotten by God.

I felt that if perchance God heard that awful wailing, then for sure I'd be rejected for my immaturity, selfishness, and lack of faith. It is possible to live a life of faith for many years, see many answers to prayers, and speak to others of God's magnificence and mercies, and then hit a wall of despair where all that is known or remembered are the old childhood wounds·and ideas about God and life. I hit that wall that afternoon.

I had tried so many plans for Mike's care, so many avenues to free up some time for myself to return to work, to ordinary life. It seemed that the hundreds of phone calls, the myriad of forms filled out and signed by doctors had all been for naught. It had gotten to the point that the obstructions to the plans were perversely miraculous. No way under normal circumstances could so many well thought-out plans fall through. It was around this time that I started writing this book to keep myself sane as I waited for my normal life to return.

OBSESSION

You start living for the obsession alone. ...You
want to arrive somewhere regardless of whether
you're enjoying the road or not. [36]

Paulo Coelho

Throughout Mike's life, if I felt like he needed
something, I'd be obsessed with it until he got it.
The obsession as he was recovering from the burn was
getting parathyroid hormone (PTH) for him. When
he was twenty-one years old—before the burn, before
he had gone to Chicago—he had been to an ophthalmologist who became alarmed when she examined his
eyes and discovered papilledema. When looking at the
back of his eye, the optic nerve looked swollen. This is
an eye finding that often indicates increased pressure
in the brain, like one would find with a brain tumor.
She sent him to a neuro-opthamologist who, after a
CAT scan of the orbits of his eyes, diagnosed him with
optic nerve drusen. He explained that there were cal-

cium deposits along his optic nerve, causing a loss of peripheral vision.

I investigated all the causes of papilledema in all those medical books that I mentioned earlier. Only now, I had more medical books and the Internet at my fingertips. One diagnostic possibility was hypoparathyroidism. I focused on hypoparathyroidism because that is a common finding with 22q.11 Deletion Syndrome.

Everyone has four little parathyroid glands imbedded in the thyroid gland. The parathyroid glands secrete parathyroid hormone (PTH). This hormone regulates the calcium and phosphorus balance in people's bodies. It probably does a lot more than that (most hormones have multiple actions), but its other actions aren't known yet.

As I read, I became convinced that that was what Mike had, and that he had probably had it his entire life. It possibly explained the airway obstruction episodes he had when he was a child, (low serum calcium can cause the airway to close). It explained the low calcium and elevated phosphorus levels found in Mike's previous lab work. Hypoparathyroidsim explained his soft and decaying teeth.

So the next time his psychiatrist wanted some labs drawn, I asked him to check his parathyroid hormone level. Sure enough, the level was too low; in addition, his serum calcium was low and the phosphorus was elevated. Because of these results, the psychiatrist referred Mike to an endocrinologist, who started Mike on the standard therapy for hypoparathyroidism, which is an active form of vitamin D and supplemental calcium. Most parents would have been content with that situation, but I wasn't. The standard therapy helps normalize calcium levels, but that is all it does. It doesn't ensure that the calcium in the body goes where it needs to be.

Hypoparathyroidism is the only human hormone deficiency condition that is not treated with the actual hormone. I reasoned that every other hormone in the human body has numerous functions and actions on different cells. Why would the parathyroid hormone be any different? At one time calcium and vitamin D supplementation was the only treatment for hypoparathyroidism. Now the hormone is available as Forteo. The FDA had approved it for treatment for osteoporosis because all the research focused on people with osteoporosis. (There is no money in using parathyroid hormone for people with hypoparathyroidism because the condition is so rare.) I would have been content with calcium and vitamin D supplementation if the hormone was not available, but now that it was on the market, I wanted Mike to have it.

I found articles in the literature about depression being a common symptom of people who develop hypoparathyroidism. There is an Internet listserv for people with hypoparathyroidism. Common complaints include depression, lack of motivation, and never quite feeling right. I reasoned that if this can happen after a short time without the hormone, could some of Mike's psychiatric illnesses be the consequence of missing the hormone for more than twenty years?

I also read about cases of hypoparathyroidism where the basal ganglia (a part of the brain) becomes calcified, and the person develops Parkinson's in their 30s. Mike had already had a hand tremor for a few years, and I didn't want it to develop into full-blown Parkinsonism. I was concerned that perhaps the calcifications that were identified in his brain on MRI were caused by the hypoparathyroidism, and I wondered if the brain calcifications were the explanation for his declining IQ over his school years. If this were true, would he continue to lose more intellectual functioning in the upcoming years?

Before the burn, while on the standard therapy for hypoparathyroidism, he had had a seizure. When taken to the ER, the labs showed a low serum calcium level. He was also dehydrated from the flu and had recently started on Seroquel—who knows if it was the low calcium levels or a combination of the above, which caused the seizure?

During the time he was in the burn unit, I realized that even in the course of a single day, his calcium levels fluctuated wildly, and his ionized calcium levels were never in the normal range. The ionized calcium is the active calcium. Even if the serum levels are normal, there is no guarantee that the active form is available to his cells. I was convinced that Mike needed this missing hormone.

His endocrinologist was reluctant to prescribe it, because it was an off-label use for the hormone. She referred him to another endocrinologist who decided that because his serum calcium levels were somewhat controlled on the current therapy that he couldn't justify its use in Mike's case because of the expense. I took him to his regular doctor, who had sent me a letter stating that a recent DEXA scan (test for bone thinning) performed by an endocrinologist after his burn had shown that Mike had osteoporosis. I hoped that perhaps she would prescribe Forteo for that. She declined. I found one more endocrinologist who did prescribe Forteo for people with hypoparathyroidism, but after another series of testing he concurred with the other two endocrinologists that Mike's calcium levels were satisfactory on the current therapy. One day I e-mailed the last endocrinologist he'd seen that I supposed I should give up this quest for parathyroid hormone for Mike, and he e-mailed back, "Yes, give it up." Randy Pausch, the famous professor who recently died of pancreatic cancer, once said, "Brick walls are there for a purpose—they let us know how badly we want things."

I tried to let go, really I did. Letting go is something that I still need lots of practice with. A week later, a notice came across my e-mail from the Hypoparathyroidism Association that the National Institutes of Health (NIH) was recruiting hypoparathyroid patients for a study using parathyroid hormone replacement therapy. The main focus of the study was the effect of the hormone on bone. Among other problems, patients with hypoparathyroidism have abnormal, very hard bones.

Mike was eligible, so the summer of 2007 we headed to NIH in Washington, D.C. to start the study. The study was designed so that the first year, he would receive standard therapy, but then the following year he'd be started on the hormone, with the option of receiving it for four more years until, hopefully, the parathyroid hormone would be approved by the FDA for use in people with hypoparathyroidism. It was the only possibility to get Mike on the hormone at the time. I was willing to do whatever it took, because I was so convinced he needed it. Mike looked at the prospect of going to NIH in Washington D.C. as a great adventure.

The National Institutes of Health is a hospital for research studies like the one Mike was on, but it is also the place where people go for last-ditch treatments for serious illnesses and cancers. It is an interesting, amazing place. Mike and I met some people who had lived there for a year or more, because it was the only place in the world where they could get the treatment they needed. Some of the people arriving on the campus for treatment looked so frail and sick it broke my heart.

The campus of the National Institutes of Health was like a college campus. It had lots of trees, buildings, grass, and hills. Since 9/11, there was a major security apparatus to get on or off campus. Just to drive in or out, the security checkpoints were much more involved than airport security. How fear can ruin things! People told me that before this security, people in the neighborhood would walk and jog on the campus because of its beautiful park-like setting. Kids would sled down the hills in the winter. However, the summer of 2007, it was locked down with security fences and security checkpoints.

I stayed in the Children's Inn, which was right on campus, while Mike stayed in his hospital room. He could order room service 24/7, which was a lot of fun for the first day or so, but that got old rather quickly. It wasn't like the room service at a fine hotel. It was, after all, hospital food. Most of the testing required for the study was easy, just blood work and urine collections. The only difficult test was the bone biopsy required by the study protocol. That required anesthesia, and Mike was sore for about a week afterward. When he wasn't getting the bone biopsy, we would spend the morning at the hospital for the tests, and in the afternoon, we'd hop on the Metro and explore Washington, D.C., usually carrying a urine jug for his twenty-four-hour urine collections.

We went up for two visits, the initial visit for a full week in the summer and then a follow-up three-day visit in January. While on the study at home, he had to follow the calcium/vitamin D regimen they put him on and get monthly labs and twenty-four-hour urines. We faithfully followed the study requirements because of the promise of finally getting the PTH hormone. The research nurse had told us stories of people getting on the hormone and how their countenances changed; they smiled more. She also told about how patients had lost motivation after having parathyroidectomies, but the motivation returned after being on the hormone for a few months. Upon hearing that, I wanted that hormone for Mike even more. Could the explanation for the lack of motivation throughout Mike's life be lack of PTH? I was so hopeful that he would feel better in his daily life and that his quality of life would improve.

He was to start on the hormone on a Monday in the middle of July. On the Friday before, as we were packing our suitcases for the drive to Washington, D.C, the telephone rang. It was the doctor in charge of the study. She called to tell us not to come, that she had cancelled the study. I asked her why, and she didn't give any reason. I hung up the phone and cried for the rest of the day. I couldn't tell anyone what had happened without crying. I cried for a few days. I found out later that she didn't really cancel the study; it is still going on now. She just dropped Mike from the study. I never found out why. Perhaps she didn't like Mike or me. Perhaps his bone thinning from the burn threw off her data.

There has been a lot of work in recent years assuring that research protocols are ethical, and that patients' rights are respected. When we signed the informed consent, it seemed like a contract stating that if we kept our end of the bargain, the researchers would be obligated to keep their end. So after she called, I read over the consent with the patient rights. Patients had the right to leave the study at any time, but there was nothing stating that if the patient has performed all the requirements for the study, they were entitled to complete the study, to get the promised medication or treatment. It seemed the two trips to Washington D.C, all the expense, all the time, all the labs, the tests, and the bone biopsy should have counted for something.

In a phone conversation with this doctor a few weeks later, she told me there would be a better study in the fall, and if that study wasn't approved, she would give Mike the PTH in her "compassionate use" study in January. I trusted the doctor to follow through with Mike. I also decided to trust God for the timing. I waited, periodically e-mailing her, reminding her that we were waiting for a date to be put either on the new study or the "compassionate use" study. One month extended into two months, until over seven months had passed. I lived those months expecting any day to get a date within a week or two. After seven months—January had come and gone—she stopped answering my e-mails about a possible date and also stopped sending the calcitriol and calcium to manage his hypoparathyroidism provided by NIH while he was on the study.

Instead of e-mails, I called her and asked her what was up. She told me that Mike was ineligible for any of her studies. By this time in my quest, there were other studies at other sites in the country looking at another form of parathyroid hormone for use with hypoparathyroid patients. None of the protocols would have worked in Mike's case, however. Again, it looked and felt like we were at the end of the line.

Because the NIH was no longer sending the calcitriol and calcium, I made an appointment with his regular doctor to get the prescriptions locally for the medications. This was a different doctor than his previous family doctor. I told him the entire story, and he believed that it was reasonable to put Mike on the parathyroid hormone. He believed, like I did, that the PTH would benefit his body in more ways than just controlling the calcium/phosphorus balance in his blood. He wrote the prescription for Forteo for Mike, believing that there would be numerous delays with insurance denials because Forteo is expensive.

I drove to the local pharmacy and obtained the Forteo for a meager co-pay of twenty-five dollars. It was that simple. After three years of searching and waiting, going from endocrinologist to endocrinologist, and following the NIH study protocol, a simple prescription, and he was on the medication. The first evening as I gave him the injection, I marveled at how simple and anticlimactic that act was.

The dose he is on is probably not large enough to adequately replace the PTH his body needs though. Mike's doctor prescribed the same dose of Forteo as people get with osteoporosis. If he were in the NIH study, he would have received three times that dose, taking it three times daily. The problem with Forteo is that its half-life is short, meaning that the hormone is only in his system a few hours. People with normal parathyroid glands have the hormone in their system all the time. Time will tell if this inadequate dose is a benefit to him. There is no way of knowing if this low dose will prevent more calcium deposits in his brain or along his optic nerve.

On his last visit to the opthamologist, we learned that the peripheral vision loss from Mike's optic nerve drusen is not getting any worse. To date, his countenance is the same, and no obvious changes in his motivation are observable. However, sometimes when he is agitated and he gives himself the shot, he calms down immediately. Lately he has been taking it in the morning before work, and they report at work that he is doing a better job at staying on task. They are currently researching a long-acting form of PTH that is specifically formulated for people with hypoparathyroidism. It should be approved within a year or two by the FDA.

JUNKYARD DOGS

I am not afraid of storms, for I am learning how
to sail my ship.[37]

Louisa May Alcott

Mike's right hand works again. It is easy to forget
that when he returned home from the hospital
he couldn't move one finger or hold his hand straight
out at the end of his arm. It had been improving slowly
on its own, but it was impossible to motivate him to
work on it so it would be entirely functional. That is,
until he dislocated his left shoulder. He is left-handed.
During the second winter after the burn, while out
drinking with his friends, he slipped on the ice and
dislocated his left shoulder.

He came into our bedroom the following morning
and first showed me a broken tooth. Then he mentioned
in passing that his shoulder was sore, and he supposed
he should rest it for a week or so. I took one look at
the deformed, dislocated shoulder and took him to

the emergency room, thinking one, two, three—the emergency doctor would pop it back in place.

Mike often had injuries in his life where his perception of pain was less than a person would expect considering the injury. I'm not sure if that is something common with 22q.11 Deletion Syndrome, or something unique to him. There probably aren't very many people who could fall asleep with a newly dislocated shoulder without seeking help. Once, when he played soccer as a youth, he broke his foot. He continued playing in the game, and it was not until the next day when his shoe was off that I noticed that his foot looked a little crooked.

Perhaps it was the burn contractures in his shoulder, or perhaps it was because he waited so long to tell me, and all the tissues in his shoulder had swelled up, but they were unable to slip his shoulder back into place in the emergency room. The emergency room doctor tried three times using conscious sedation. This particular emergency room is close to some ski slopes, and this doctor told me that during the winter he pops dislocated shoulders back in place daily. He met his nemesis with Mike's shoulder though. He tried all the tricks he knew. I knew we were in trouble when he got out his orthopedic textbooks and used them as guides to set up some contraptions with pulleys and weights. When even that didn't work, he called in an orthopedic surgeon who also was unsuccessful.

They transferred Mike to another hospital where he was taken to surgery to put his shoulder back in place under deep anesthesia. Once surgery was over, one of the great-big orthopedic residents, a football type, waddled out of the OR, and whispered in a high squeaky voice to the nurse, "I think I got a hernia." I am glad I wasn't in that OR watching them wrestle his shoulder back in place.

Mike was required to keep that shoulder immobilized for a month. He had physical therapy after that for a few months. After a few months of therapy, when he still wasn't able to raise his left arm, we realized that he had sustained a rotator cuff tear It may have been caused from the dislocation itself or perhaps by the heroic force needed to get it back in place while he was under anesthesia that day. Regardless of the cause, it needed repair. It took at least four months, from the time of the dislocation until after surgery, before he could start using his left arm and hand again. During those months, he was forced to use his right hand for everything. That was just the therapy that right hand needed!

The orthopedic surgeon who operated on his rotator cuff tear had a son who played football on the same team as Mike in high school. He remembered Mike. When he walked into the exam room for the shoulder consult, and saw Mike with his scarred face, chest and arms, missing ears, the gimpy right hand, the tilted posture from the burn contractures in his neck, and his disheveled clothes, he laughed and kidded him, "Mike, you are a junkyard dog!" I looked at Mike and thought to myself, *I guess he really looks uglier than a junkyard dog.* Mike laughed. It sounded terrible, but he took it as a compliment. He had been through a lot and had the scars to show for it. He was tougher than nails, a survivor.

Sometimes when I look at Mike these days, I think I am really seeing him, maybe for the first time, just as he is: a junkyard dog, who is also vulnerable and sensitive and needing so much love and affection. There were many years when I would look at Mike and not see him. I would see my fears for his future, I would see his lacks and struggles, and in his difficulties and deficiencies, see my own bad mothering. Even after a half hour of primping (by me)—he still looks disheveled, or will miraculously become disheveled in a matter of minutes. His clothes are magnets for dirt and spills of every sort. He crushes the heels of his shoes because he is too lazy to put them on correctly. His pants always drag the ground, his underwear showing out the back. His fly is never up. These days I can look at him, the entire picture, and smile with such love and affection. I love him just as he is, and always will. I still try to straighten out his clothes, but the angst is gone.

I suppose the years have changed me also, perhaps making me a junkyard dog in my own right. I have my own battle scars. This journey has made me tough. I used to care so much about how things looked and what people thought about me. Now I find there is no need to hide anything, or pretend that things are different from what they are. I am comfortable with inconsistencies, contradictions and imperfection. I am enjoying what is, as it is, grateful for the scraps sent my way.

Note the occupational therapy for his right hand

DIFFERENT BATTLEFIELDS

I drink not from mere joy in wine nor to scoff at faith—no, only to forget myself for a moment, that only do I want from intoxication, that alone.[38]

Omar Khayyam, 11th century Persian mathematician, astronomer, philosopher and poet

When I first started writing this book during Mike's early recovery, I had hopes of a nice, clean, happy ending where Mike is healed and happy and readers could close the book with a smile. I was hoping for a newfound faith for Mike, where he walked through all his days with a certain deep knowledge of God's love for him. If I am going to tell the truth though, few things in this life are perfect or end perfectly. To live is to struggle.

A major struggle these days is that he smokes. Almost every person with a psychiatric illness smokes. When my husband and I were nursing students in the late 1970s, the psychiatric wards of hospitals were the smokiest places in the world. The hallways and community rooms of psychiatric hospitals were filled with a smoky cigarette haze.

Nicotine is one of the most addictive substances known to man. Humans are born with nicotine receptors in their bodies. It is very difficult for the average person to quit smoking, but so much more difficult for someone who struggles with a psychiatric disorder. Not only is nicotine addictive, but it also helps ameliorate many psychiatric symptoms.[39] Some research shows that nicotine helps a person with psychiatric illness concentrate better, think more clearly, and be more sociable. Instead of wasting research dollars immorally exploring ways to make cigarettes more addictive, cigarette companies should instead be investigating the pharmaceutical potential of nicotine for treating psychiatric symptoms and finding ways to deliver the medication in a manner that is non-addicting, without the health hazards.

On one level, I understand that Mike is not only addicted, but he is self-medicating. On a thousand other levels, I hate the fact that he smokes. The only problem Mike sees with smoking is that he runs out of money too quickly. The problem that he doesn't see is that the cigarettes are eating away his already damaged lungs from the deletion, the pneumonias, the burn, and the ARDS. After the burn, his pulmonologist diagnosed him with only 40-percent lung function left. When he smokes, he coughs, wheezes, and gets short of breath just walking. I do not like this recurring breathing problem in his life.

Smoking is accelerating and compounding all the previous damage to his lungs. There is nothing I can do to make him quit. I have taken him to smoking cessation classes, but he'd be outside smoking cigarettes while I'd be sitting in class trying to be attentive to everything I already knew. If I could choose for him, he would have strong lungs for every breath he takes in this life, and he would have millions of easy breaths left to breathe. It is not my choice though. I fret about a future where he will have to carry an oxygen tank around to get the oxygen he needs.

His coughing makes me gag, and his shortness of breath tears my insides. When he runs out of money for cigarettes, he wanders the streets and hangs around gas stations and bars in hopes of scoring a cigarette or a dollar off someone. When that doesn't work, he has been observed picking up discarded cigarette butts on the sidewalk and smoking them. This is not exactly a mother's dream for her son. So if you perchance encounter a young man with some scars and disheveled clothes panhandling for money or cigarettes, do not let your compassion get the better of you. Look at him sternly and tell him he must quit smoking.

> I really do want to quit smoking. It will save a lot of money. I will be free then. I really want to do that, but I have no willpower sometimes. One cigarette leads to another. Somehow, I need to come up with a good plan. The odds of me quitting smoking are pretty bad. The

Jacksonville Jaguars will win the Super Bowl, before I am able to quit.

Mike

The other issue is alcohol. Mike is not only missing some key genes on chromosome 22 but since both my husband and I both come from long lines of alcoholics, I am sorry to say he is probably the unlucky recipient of some alcoholic genes that are not located on the q arm, band 11 of chromosome 22. Perhaps the alcohol provides an escape from his day-to-day struggles, from his disabilities. He feels freer and talks more easily when he has some alcohol in his system.

As his parents, we have devised a multitude of schemes to help him stop:

We pray a lot.

We discuss it with his psychiatrist at every visit.

We try not to give him any money.

We encourage attendance at Alcoholics Anonymous (AA) meetings. Sometimes he is willing to attend, but only the meetings that permit smoking. The only visible benefit he gains from attendance is a pocketful of cigarettes he has bummed from the other attendees.

We have attempted to get him into local alcohol rehab programs and hit the same walls of lack of programs for people with developmental disabilities that we encountered when looking for drug rehab programs in high school.

We are powerless. He likes his alcohol.

His friends from high school care a lot about him and are trying to get him to quit.

We live close to Akron, the birthplace of Alcoholics Anonymous. There is good treatment and a lot of hope for this disease. In fact, some of the healthiest and holiest people I know are recovered alcoholics. Mike isn't ready to quit and has not acknowledged his need for AA yet. His developmental disability might interfere with his full engagement with the twelve steps of AA because they require some abstract thought. We will see.

One night he came home smashed to the point where he could not stand. I was scared to see him so drunk, having learned of the dangers of alcohol poisoning when I worked in college health. Hundreds of college students die from it every year. I called 911, knowing he needed observation and IV hydration. Where we currently live, they only have a volunteer fire department, and no one was available, so the police called an ambulance from the neighboring town, where we used to live.

When the ambulance arrived, I greeted the same paramedic who had transported him so many times in his life since he was an infant. It had been four years since the last ambulance ride for the burn. The paramedic still had the same kind smile and quiet manner. He saw us, smiled, and said, "Hi, nice to see you again." I smiled back sheepishly, wondering what he was thinking about all the predicaments that he had rescued us from during the past quarter of a century. We helped Mike stumble on to the stretcher. I grabbed my purse, a jacket, and a book, prepared for another stay in another emergency room.

Normal Enough

We all live in the world with a sense of normalcy, a belief that things are a certain way and that there is some predictability to life. And this is largely true. Grass grows long and green instead of in purple squares, and the sun appears and disappears every day. So in a sense there is some predictability to life, but that predictability belies the immense mystery that is all around us.[40]

Christopher S Kilham

During the initial writing phase of this book, I was wondering how to end it on the day of the alcohol poisoning incident. It seemed like a clever ending…beginning the book with an ambulance ride and finishing it with one, especially since it was the same paramedic who had been around for all of Mike's crises. However, during the years that this book lay dormant on the hard drive of my computer, life has continued to unfold. It may have been a clever ending, but not a true ending. That was just a bad day. Sometimes miracles take a few years.

Mike works everyday now in Hattie's Café close to our house. It is a combination sandwich shop and gift shop. It was started by the Hattie Larlham Foundation. Dennis Allen, the CEO had a vision many years ago of having businesses run by and for people with developmental disabilities. He started with this shop, but now there are five other shops like it in the county. They also have a few doggie day care centers and they run the county animal protective league. To supply the café there is an organic garden and a bakery where people with developmental disabilities work.

Mike loves his job at Hattie's, and the people there love him. In all my frenzy to find a job and plan a future for him, I never dreamed that he would have a position that he enjoyed so much, where he could continue to learn and grow. It is a wonderful place, and the managers/job coaches are so kind. He is celebrating his five year anniversary at that job this year.

Mike has moved out of our home and now lives in a supported living apartment with another disabled gentleman around four miles from our house. He and his roommate are friends and they care for each other. His roommate has troubles expressing himself, but Mike can understand him and make him laugh. He has always been a sensitive person, but I have noticed a new awareness of and compassion for those who suffer. When he sees other people with disabilities, he goes out of his way to be friendly and kind to them. This wasn't always the case. All through grade school and high school he snubbed the other students in his special education classes. He no longer makes a distinction between someone who is disabled and not.

He still has a wonderful laugh and loves teasing people and joking around. He is more communicative, and expressive of his thoughts and feelings. He also has grown to be a man that people enjoy talking to and feel comfortable confiding in. It took him a little longer to mature than his peers but it is happening. I am starting to view him these days not as my child any more, but as a companion and friend. I enjoy his company.

There is a pub within walking distance of his apartment that he frequents often. He knows many of the regulars, the waitresses, and bartenders. They greet him when he walks in. When he is out of money, someone usually buys him a beer or two. His drinking and smoking continue to be issues. Overall though, he is making better decisions.

He also wants to keep learning. For six months or so he was bugging me about going back to school. I finally got him into a tutoring program. They have identified that he is functioning on a sixth grade level. They are starting at that level with the basics. This is the first time in his life he has been motivated to really study and learn. He gets tutoring twice a week and does homework in between. We are not sure where it will lead, but we are taking things day by day.

Since the burn, Mike has been hospitalized two more times for mania and psychosis. Actually it was just one episode divided into two hospitalizations. In the first hospitalization for mania, he was so anxious to be discharged he convinced the psychiatrist to discharge him before he was really better and he landed back in the hospital a week later in psychosis. Hospitalizations for psychosis are heart rending. It breaks my heart seeing him out of his right mind. Each hospitalization is less scary than the previous one though. We have a history under our belts of seeing him recover completely. The psychosis is short-lived thank God. He has a lot of insight into his illness. He is able to identify his feelings better and ask for help when they get out of control. He lets people know now if he is feeling so bad he wants to hurt himself.

We have had to switch psychiatrists a few more times, changing now only because the psychiatrists have moved on to greener pastures. We have been part of NAMI, the local organization for the National Alliance for the Mentally Ill, and have discovered that the best way to find a good psychiatrist is through word of mouth. He also receives counseling once a week. The counselors change frequently also, but he is learning different things from each one.

The nerve damage to Mike's feet from the burn that caused foot drop when he was in the hospital has healed completely. He no longer walks with his feet slapping the floor with each step. The itching still occurs, but it is rare, and I suspect it wouldn't even be a problem if he would put moisturizing cream on his torso. He is covered with burn scars, but each year the scars are suppler, less red, and blend in with the rest of his skin. His face and lips are less distorted. His face is starting to look like his old face again, with the scars mostly localized to the cheeks and chin. If you look at him at a certain angle in a certain light, the scars could pass for a five o'clock shadow. I am waiting for the day to come when his skin looks like that of the lady that used to come and visit him in the hospital, where you could hardly tell she had been burned.

As patients with kidney disease start dialysis, we talk about them getting used to a "new normal." I don't think living with 22q.11 Deletion Syndrome means adjusting to a new normal, because there was never an old normal. Our lives are normal enough though. We have all learned an acceptance of the reality of what is with all its problems, imperfections and abnormalities, even when it is crazy, even when it seems things are out of control. There are always issues to be addressed. We deal with them the best we can, knowing and accepting them as part of the journey, always grateful for Mike's life.

Even with all the sorrows and difficulties, life is good. That old fear that started when he stopped breathing in my arms as a baby is gone. It is not that I don't know that bad things can still happen. Maybe it is because I think I have finally come to the realization that after years of trying to protect him (unsuccessfully, the reader might affirm), I am more powerless than I would like to believe. I can't control much or really protect Mike from anything, so why worry? I have learned that God is present in the midst of crisis and suffering. I would even go so far to say that he is more present—closer when it seems the world is falling apart. He suffers with us. He continues to be closer to me than I am to myself. In the end, that is all that matters. I have learned in a deep way that God is good, and his mercy is everlasting. He never promised that there wouldn't be suffering or pain or sorrow in this world. But he did promise that he would be with us, and his mercy would follow us all the days of our life. One day after another, one step after another. He is near.

> I really want people to like me for who I am. That's all I ever wanted. I like it when people give me compliments. I like to be around my friends and I like to have money. One day I would like to have a girlfriend and maybe one day I would like to have a family. I would like to raise a baby someday. I am really happy where I am at now. I have a nice family.

> My apartment is really cool. I have my own room with a TV in it. I have Chris Horton my roommate, and Tricia, my house manager and I really like them.

I have a job at Hattie's Café. My job is going pretty good right now. I sweep and mop the floor. I am a food runner, I bus tables, and wash the dishes sometime. I have so much love in my life. I am happy. The burn really changed my life. It made me appreciate my life.

My life is headed in the right direction. I want to share my story. I am a survivor. When people look at me now, I hope they see that I am an image of God. I want to help people feel good about themselves. I know that God saved my life and I want to do anything I can to save people from being suicidal. I want to put a smile on peoples' faces. It makes me happy when other people are happy.

Mike

The Busch Men circa 2012

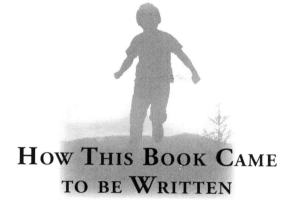

How This Book Came
to be Written

Human beings only create by drawing on their poverty.[41]

Brother Roger of Taize

I started writing this book during Mike's recuperation from the burn at home before I returned to work. I wrote during those months when I couldn't find a nurse for Mike, couldn't arrange transportation to rehab, and couldn't figure out a job or way for him to fill his days while I was working. While frustrated with all the waiting, I started figuring that perhaps the reason for all the obstructions and little pockets of free time when Mike was in rehab was that now was the time to start writing. I understood in a cosmic sense that God had "grounded" me. I was not to be to "let out of my room" until I had at least started this book. I started writing under duress, with the hope that once the book was started, there would be a return to normal life. (After reading this book though, the reader might be asking himself or herself just exactly what I think "normal" might be.)

The suspicion that God had grounded me, divinely commissioning me to write this book, did not immunize me against the daily battles with busyness, insecurities, laziness, and squandering hours on the Internet. It was difficult to silence the inner critic mumbling repeatedly,

You are wasting your time.

You're whining too much.

You told the story all wrong.

Who would fritter away his or her time reading this drivel?

It was difficult to write when the kitchen was a mess or the health department would have condemned the bathroom. It was impossible to write when the weather was beautiful, and the sun and the wind were calling me outside to play. Luckily for this book, I live in the Cleveland, Ohio area, and clear balmy days are the exception rather than the rule.

After returning to work, life became very busy, and this book gathered dust on the hard drive of my computer for a few years while we returned to the wonderful daily rhythm of ordinary life. This book may have been forgotten entirely, but then menopause hit. For me, menopause is synonymous with middle-of-the-night insomnia. Some internal biological clock aberration routinely started awakening me in the middle of the night for an hour or so. Instead of lying awake uselessly in bed,

I dusted off the book and started working on it again, while the house was asleep and the phone was silent. Many of the early chapters of this book were gleaned from old journals. Instead of memory books, when my sons were born, I started writing a journal for each of them to remind them of the stories of their childhood.

Writing the story down was part of the healing process of all that we had been through. I wrote many of the chapters as tears flowed down my cheeks; I remembered again and again how much I loved Mike. I saw how my faith had changed over the years. At one time, I thought I could predict how God would answer a particular prayer or intervene in a certain situation, (or at least thought I knew how he *should* intervene). Now I know truly that as far as the heavens are above the earth so are his thoughts above our thoughts and ways above our ways (Isaiah 55:9). I have been blessed by God's unexpected presence and strength in the darkest moments. In addition, I have learned that I do not want to live a moment on this earth without grace and mercy, and never want the Holy Spirit to be taken from me.

22q.11 Deletion Syndrome: A Basic Primer

Human genes not only determine physical characteristics like the hair color and sex of individuals, but also heavily impact personality, including whether a person will like music or art or nature or machines. Chromosomes also direct the development, growth, reproductive, and dying processes of living beings. In humans, chromosomes are diploid, double-stranded. One strand comes from the mother; the other strand comes from the father. These pairs of chromosomes are numbered from 1 to 23. A single chromosome contains thousands of genes. Every person has 2 copies of the same gene, but there can be a multitude of variations for each particular gene, called alleles.

For a single cell to divide, chromosomes go through a process of completely replicating themselves as the cell divides. In a human, this consists of at least twenty-three thousand protein-coding genes rearranging themselves in the same order every time a cell divides. Each of these twenty-three thousand genes has thousands of base pairs that usually match up perfectly every time. The process of cell division happens millions of times in a single human in a single day. Try to wrap your brain around those numbers.

Chromosomes also divide and rearrange themselves during reproduction. In the process of creating sperm and eggs, cells divide twice, shuffling the genes or alleles between the parental chromosomes, resulting in single-stranded chromosomes in eggs and sperm with a totally unique combination of the various alleles. During conception, these two very different cells unite their single-stranded chromosomes together to become a new human zygote. Miraculously, most of the time, these processes happen perfectly, without a single hitch. Errors are rare, but they do happen occasionally. Sometimes there is a deletion of genetic material, but duplications, translocations, inversions, insertions, and the development of rings are also possible. The location and extent of the error on the chromosome determines what kind of effect it will have on the person.

Chromosome 22 is the smallest of the human chromosomes and has the honor of being the first chromosome to be completely sequenced in December 1999. Before 1993, if a child was born with a small deletion of the long arm of this chromosome, if the child was diagnosed at all, he or she may have been labeled as having either Velocardiofacial syndrome (VCFS), DiGeorge syndrome, Shprintzen syndrome, Craniofacial syndrome, or Conotruncal Anomaly Unusual Face

Syndrome (CTAF). A syndrome is a disease or disorder that has more than one identifying feature. Syndromes get named because a specialist in a certain field of medicine, after seeing a number of children with similar characteristics, describes the syndrome and then names it (often after himself).

Prior to the recent genetic revolution, child specialists would resort to paging through syndrome books when presented with a funny-looking kid with odd symptoms. They were hoping to match the child's face and symptoms to the syndrome, and then use the diagnosis to provide guidance for the parents. In recent decades, syndrome books have been replaced with genetic testing to identify the chromosome defects causing the various syndromes. 22q.11 Deletion Syndrome is just one of many genetic syndromes that a child can be born with.

There are two terms frequently used in genetics. The first term is genotype and it describes the genetic configuration in a person. Phenotype describes the effects or manifestations of the genetic configuration. One genotype can generate a variety of phenotypes. Children with Down syndrome have such a characteristic phenotype that they are easily identified. On the other hand, the phenotype for children with 22q.11 Deletion Syndrome can be quite variable. This is one reason why 22q.11 Deletion Syndrome is frequently missed and has so many syndromes named after it.

Close to two hundred problems or physical characteristics have been identified with 22q.11 Deletion

Syndrome. A cardiac problem is the most commonly shared manifestation. Another very common structural problem is cleft lip or cleft palate. This can interfere with speech development and cause feeding problems. Other common manifestations include small thymuses and undeveloped parathyroid glands. The thymus abnormality can cause immune problems, and the undeveloped parathyroid glands cause problems in calcium regulation in the body. There are numerous other physical problems, which can include small or malformed kidneys, clubfeet, missing or kinked arteries, jugular vein abnormalities, various hernias, malrotation of the bowel, anal anomalies, small hands and feet, extra fingers, scoliosis, and vertebral problems.

In addition to physical abnormalities, developmental and learning difficulties emerge as the child grows. Each stage of development brings unique challenges for both the child and the parents in dealing with them. Common problems encountered in infancy include: poor growth, feeding difficulties, constipation, frequent infections, irritability, poor muscle tone, and delayed attainment of developmental milestones.

As a child with this deletion develops, many of the physical problems become less of an issue and social and educational concerns move to the forefront. Over ninety percent of these children have some sort of learning disorder, and many also struggle with a low or borderline IQ. During the school years, a child with the deletion usually learns to read but often struggles with mathematical concepts and reading comprehension. They will always have great difficulty with abstract thinking. Disabilities in social interactions and understanding social cues often emerge during these years.

Adolescence brings with it different problems and issues. The exact percentage isn't known, but many individuals with this deletion develop psychiatric illnesses in childhood, adolescence, and early adulthood. The incidence peaks during adolescence. The missing genes along the stretch of 22q.11 are responsible for making some important enzymes involved in the regulation of key brain neurotransmitters. Too much or too little of these neurotransmitters is what leads to mood disorders and psychosis. Some common diagnoses found in the syndrome include bipolar disorder, schizoaffective disorder, schizophrenia, obsessive-compulsive disorder, attention deficit disorder, and phobias. There is much current ongoing research regarding mental illness and 22q.11 Deletion Syndrome. To date, it is the only known genetic cause of mental illness. If the reader is interested in gaining more knowledge and insight about 22q.11 Deletion Syndrome, a few good websites are listed at the back of the book.

RECOMMENDED READING

Missing Genetic Pieces. Strategies for Living with VCFS. By Sherry Baker-Gomez (2004). Desert Pearl Publishing. Glendale, Arizona.

Educating Children with Velo-Cardio-Facial Syndrome. By Donna Cutler-Landsman (2007). Plural Publishing. San Diego, California

Footprints of Hope. By Raymond Tanner (2004). Freestyle Publications. Seaford, South Australia.

WEBSITES

www.22qcentral.com

www.22crew.org

http://dempsterfamilyfoundation.org/

http://ghr.nlm.nih.gov/condition=22q112deletionsyndrome

http://22q.org

www.ncbi.nlm.nih.gov/bookshelf/br.fcgi?book=gene&part=gr_22q11deletion

http://rarediseases.info.nih.gov/gard/disease.aspx?pageid=4&diseaseid=10299

www.c22c.org/vcfs.htm

http://www.ucdmc.ucdavis.edu/mindinstitute/videos/video_22q.html

http://www.friendsofquinn.com/

OTHER BURN STORIES

The Burn Journals. By Brent Runyon (2004). Alfred A.
Knopf. New York, NY.

Joel by Joel Sonnenberg with Gregg Lewis. (2004).
Zondervan. Grand Rapids, Nichigan

ENDNOTES

1   Inward/Outward, "Meister Eckhart." Last modified 2012. Accessed October 29, 2012. http://www.inwardoutward.org/author/meister-eckhart.

2   Wiesel, Elie., The Gates of the Forest. Holt, Rinehart and Winston 1966

3   Karen Blixen-Isak Dinesen Information Site, "Your Questions." Last modified 2001. Accessed October 29, 2012. http://www.karenblixen.com/question42.html.

4   Goodreads, "Martin Buber Quotes." Accessed October 29, 2012. http://www.goodreads.com/quotes/2858-all-journeys-have-secret-destinations-of-which-the-traveler-is.

5   C.S. Lewis Daily, "First 75 Quotes from Twitter.com/CSLewisDaily." Accessed October 29, 2012. http://cslewisdaily.blogspot.com/2009/09/first-75-quotes-from.html.

6   Kushner, H.S. When Bad Things Happen to Good People. Avon Books, HarperCollins Publishers, New York. 1981.

7   Quotations Book, "Rilke, Ranier Maria." Accessed October 29, 2012. http://quotationsbook.com/quote/23828/.

8   Goodreads, "L. Frank Baum Quotes." Accessed October 29, 2012. http://www.goodreads.com/quotes/126641-whenever-i-feel-blue-i-start-breathing-again.

9   Famous Literary Works, "For Whom the Bell Tolls." Accessed October 29, 2012. http://www.famousliteraryworks.com/donne_for_whom_the_bell_tolls.htm.

10 Vaqas , Asghar. "Cure the disease and kill the patient." The Express Tribune , August 01, 2011. http://blogs.tribune.com.pk/story/7368/cure-the-disease-and-kill-the-patient/ (accessed October 29, 2012).

11 All Poetry, "Colored Toys by Rabindranath Tagore." Accessed October 29, 2012. http://allpoetry.com/poem/8516551-Colored_Toys-by-Rabindranath_Tagore.

12 Donley, C. and Buckley, S. eds.(1996) The Tyranny of the Normal, An Anthology. The Kent State University Press, Kent, Ohio.

13 Gothelf, D, Lombroso, P.J. "Genetics of Childhood Disorders; XXV Velocardiofacial Syndrome." Journal of the American Academy of Psychiatry, 40, 489-491. April 2001.

14 Feinstein, C., and Eliez, S. "The Velocardiofacial Syndrome in Psychiatry." "Current Opinion in Psychiatry." 13: 485-490

15 Rohr, R., Radical Grace: Daily Meditations by Richard Rohr , St Anthony Press, Cincinnati, Oh. 1995. p 304

16 AZLyrics, "Leonard Cohen Lyrics." Accessed October 29, 2012. http://www.azlyrics.com/lyrics/leonardcohen/anthem.html.

17 Singer, "Taking Life: Humans," Excerpted from Practical Ethics, 2nd edition, Cambridge University Press, 1993, pp. 175-217.

18 Mother Theresa. (1995). A Simple Path. Balantine Books, New York, New York.

19 Beck, M., (1999). Expecting Adam; A True Story of Birth, Rebirth, and Everyday Magic. Berkely Books. New York, New York.

20 Goodreads, "Steve Martin Quotes." Accessed October 29, 2012. http://www.goodreads.com/quotes/368701-i-used-to-smoke-marijuana-but-i-ll-tell-you-something.

21 ThinkExist.com, "Gilda Radner Quotes." Accessed October 29, 2012. http://thinkexist.com/quotation/life_is_about_not_knowing-having_to_change-taking/207745.html.

22 Bartleby.com, "Emily Dickinson Complete Poems." Accessed October 29, 2012. http://www.bartleby.com/113/2089.html.

23 Quotations Book, "Elbert Hubbard." Accessed October 29, 2012. http://quotationsbook.com/quote/40373/.

24 Grief Speaks, "Traumatic and Sudden Loss." Accessed October 29, 2012. http://www.griefspeaks.com/id107.html.

25 Tree of Lives, "Lord, Hear My Prayers." Last modified 2012. Accessed October 30, 2012. http://www.google.com/url?sa=t&rct=j&q=&esrc=s&source=web&cd=2&ved=0CCkQFjAB&url=http://www.treeoflives.org/category/aids/home-visits/&ei=7F6PUMceW82wWlx4GgCA&usg=AFQjcejSE-UNiSp_GFbyFQ9B_YNjCC_g.

26 Olshansky, S. (1962). Chronic sorrow: A response to having a mentally defective child. Social Casework, 43(4), 190-193.

27 Brainy Quote, "Pedro Almodovar Quotes." Accessed October 30, 2012. Hospitals are places that you have to stay in for a long time, even if you are a visitor. Time doesn't seem to pass in the same way in hospitals as it does in other places. Pedro Almodovar.

28 Study English Today, "Emily Dickinson." Last modified 2005. Accessed October 30, 2012. http://www.studyenglishtoday.net/dickinson.html.

29 IndiaDivine.org, "Rabindranath Tagore- akhari kavita(the last poem) ." Last modified 2008. Accessed October 30, 2012. http://www.

indiadivine.org/audarya/vedic-verses/450273-rabindranath-tagore-akhari-kavita-last-poem. html.

30 ThinkExist.com, "Albert Einstein Quotes." Accessed October 30, 2012. http://thinkexist. com/quotation/a_question_that_sometimes_ drives_me_hazy-am_i_or/327434.html.

31 Hello Poetry, "W.H. Auden." Last modified 2012. Accessed October 30, 2012. http:// hellopoetry.com/-w-h-auden/chatter/?page=5.

32 Quotations Book, "Henry Wadsworth Longfellow." Accessed October 30, 2012. http:// quotationsbook.com/quote/15528/.

33 Quote Garden, "Quotations about Attitude." Last modified 2012. Accessed October 30, 2012. http://www.quotegarden.com/attitude.html.

34 Brainy Quote, "Anton Chekhov Quotes." Last modified 2012. Accessed October 30, 2012. http://www.brainyquote.com/quotes/quotes/a/ antonchekh161769.html.

35 The Mark Twain House & Museum, "Famous Twain Quotes." Accessed October 30, 2012. http://www.marktwainhouse.org/man/famous_ twain_quotes.php.

36 ThinkExist.com, "Paulo Coelho Quotes." Last modified 2012. Accessed October 30, 2012. http://thinkexist.com/quotation/you-start-living-for-the-obsession-alone-you-want/557101.html.

37 Goodreads, "Louisa May Alcott Quotes." Last modified 2012. Accessed October 30, 2012. http://www.goodreads.com/quotes/19092-i-am-not-afraid-of-storms-for-i-am-learning.

38 Thoughtsfortheday.org, Last modified 2010. Accessed December 10, 2012. http://www.thoughtsfortheday.org/category/misc.

39 Lyon, E. R. A Review of the Effects of Nicotine on Schizophrenia and Antipsychotic Medications. Psychiatr Serv, Oct 1999; 50: 1346 - 1350.

40 Kilham, Christopher S (2011). The Five Tibetans. Healing Arts Press, Rochester, Vermont

41 Exploring the Kingdom-Quote and Snippets, "Discovering Taize, August 20, 1940." Last modified 2011. Accessed October 30, 2012. http://etk-quotes.blogspot.com/.

25129530R00180

Made in the USA
Columbia, SC
28 August 2018